God's grace and
Abound in your life.
Love!
Teresa

Conquering Strongholds

Free to be who God Created You to Be

By
Minister Teresia Dupins

AuthorHouse™
1663 Liberty Drive, Suite 200
Bloomington, IN 47403
www.authorhouse.com
Phone: 1-800-839-8640

© *2009 Minister Teresia Dupins. All rights reserved.*

No part of this book may be reproduced, stored in a retrieval system, or transmitted by any means without the written permission of the author.

First published by AuthorHouse 12/4/2009

ISBN: 978-1-4490-5098-6 (e)
ISBN: 978-1-4490-5096-2 (sc)

Library of Congress Control Number: 2009912175

Printed in the United States of America
Bloomington, Indiana

This book is printed on acid-free paper.

DEDICATION

To my Heavenly Father, Jesus Christ and the Holy Spirit for giving me the grace and wisdom to write this book.

To my dear, wonderful husband, Prentice Dupins Sr., who has always believed I could accomplish great things by the grace of God. He demonstrates a spirit of excellence in ministry that motivates me to glorify God with my life.

To my dear cousin, Carolyn Cato Colclough, who partners with me in ministry. Her passion for the Lord inspires me.

To my four sisters (Phyllis, Berhonda, Herschelia and Gigi) who spoke the truth to me in love and helped me face challenges in my life.

To my parents, family, friends and spiritual mentors, who instilled in me a desire to serve God with my whole heart.

ACKNOWLEDGMENTS

Special thanks to my editor, Helaine R. Williams of The Umoja Network, for her prayers, expert advice and encouragement.

Special thanks to my children, Amanda and Prentice Jr.; daughter-in-law Katrina; and grandson Zachary, all of whom I want to leave a legacy.

Special thanks to my church family, Covenant Family Church, for their prayers and support.

PREFACE

This book was inspired by God to help Christians learn how to conquer strongholds in their lives. Strongholds prevent Christians from walking in freedom — the freedom God predestined for them before the foundations of the world. The Bible says in Colossians 1:13 that "**[the Father] has delivered and drawn us to Himself out of the control and dominion of darkness and has transferred us into the Kingdom of the Son of His love**" (Amplified Bible). In this verse, God is clearly saying that born-again Christians have been delivered from the power and control of darkness (sin and sinful thoughts and behaviors). In many instances, however, Christians are still in bondage to their fleshly desires and thought patterns. Christians may appear to "have it all together" on the outside but, on the inside, struggle with sins that block their spiritual growth. Not only is their spiritual growth hindered; their fellowship with the Lord, and effectiveness in ministry, suffers also.

You may be wondering, "What are strongholds and how do they develop in a person's life?" This book will answer these questions and many more. I will also share my personal struggle with strongholds and how I was delivered from them. I am now walking in the freedom God predestined for me in this life. Freedom from strongholds has given me the ability to be a victorious Christian — even during times of adversity. Now, God's power is flowing through me, enabling me to minister and be a blessing to others. It is my desire to help other Christians conquer strongholds so that God's power can be manifested in their lives and ministries.

Contents

Introduction	**xiii**
I Understanding Strongholds	
Chapter 1. What Are Strongholds?	1
Chapter 2. The Origin of Strongholds	7
Chapter 3. The Lie: How Strongholds Entered the Human Race	11
II Where Strongholds Reside	
Chapter 4. Our Thought Life: A Seed is Planted	15
Chapter 5. The Development of Strongholds in the Mind	19
Chapter 6. The Mind: The Stronghold's Battleground	25
Chapter 7. The Flesh: The Stronghold's Attachment and Root	29
III Identifying Strongholds in Your Life	
Chapter 8. God's Predestined Plan	35
Chapter 9. Identifying Thoughts and Beliefs That Oppose the Word of God	41
Chapter 10. Come out of Darkness into the Marvelous Light	45
IV: How to Conquer Strongholds	
Chapter 11. Programming Your New Nature and Renewing Your Mind	57
Chapter 12. Deleting Old Sinful Data	61
Chapter 13. Entering New Data: The Word of God	65
V Making God Your Only Stronghold	
Chapter 14. Delighting Yourself in the Lord	71
Chapter 15. Living Holy and Righteously	75
Bibliography	**83**
About the Author	**85**

INTRODUCTION

This book was ordained by God to help Christians conquer strongholds and walk in truth and victory. Basically, strongholds are habitual thoughts, behaviors, lifestyles and beliefs that disagree with the Word of God. Your decision to read this book indicates that you have an interest in strongholds, or desire freedom from them. You may also recognize the existence of issues in your life that are not pleasing to God and prevent you from growing in Christ. For many years, I had problems with ungodly thought patterns about which I was too ashamed to tell anyone. I feared being judged or ridiculed by others if I shared what was really going on in my mind and heart. As a result, I remained in bondage to negative thought patterns and mindsets. This prevented me from truly enjoying my relationship with the Lord and seeking Him with my whole heart. Psalm 104:34 perfectly expresses how every believer's relationship with God should be: **"May my meditation be sweet to Him; as for me, I will rejoice in the Lord"** (Amplified Bible). At times, I had difficulty rejoicing in the Lord because I knew my negative and ungodly thought patterns were not pleasing or "sweet" to Him. I attended church practically every Sunday, but negative, vain, and fleshly thoughts dominated my mind. In essence, I was not free to be the woman God had predestined me to be.

In 1997, my husband informed me that God had called him to pastor a church. The Holy Spirit impressed upon my spirit that my husband needed a strong, godly wife to support him in ministry. This is when I truly began to desire to live a holy life in spirit, soul (mind, will and emotions), and body. Eventually, I made the choice to renew (make new) my mind with the Word of God by meditating on scriptures, listening to teaching tapes, and reading books. Renewing my mind was the first step to conquering strongholds in my life.

My past and current experiences in ministry have revealed to me that many Christians struggle with living a life that is pleasing to God. In numerous instances, mental strongholds are preventing people from living holy lives and experiencing victory. Countless Spirit-filled Christians attend church every Sunday and look fabulous on the outside, but on the inside, their souls are in bondage to sinful behaviors and thought patterns.

Let's look at the following scenarios involving a few fictitious characters. Each scenario gives a clear example of strongholds and bondage in the life of a Christian.

Pastor Glover had a long time vision from God of preaching to hundreds of people in a large church. Ten years after he began Steps of Jesus Ministries International in a rural barn, he now preaches three services per Sunday in a state-of-the-art sanctuary that seats 10,000; serves as senior pastor of a staff of 50 associate pastors; and has a popular radio and television ministry. Pastor Glover also has a beautiful family consisting of a wife and twin daughters. What people don't know, however, is that Pastor Glover has fallen prey to a stronghold of womanizing ... which has led to adultery. What began innocently as 5-10 minute counseling sessions with women about serious problems in their lives eventually became sexual affairs. Pastor Glover knows what he's doing is wrong; he desperately wants to stop. But the urge to continue the affairs is so strong, he always ends up rationalizing them away ... until the next time he finds himself sobbing on the floor in regret. When Pastor Glover's sinful acts were exposed, he was removed as pastor of the ministry with which God had blessed him.

Polly had a difficult childhood partially due to being raised by an alcoholic, poverty-stricken single mother. Vowing to create a better life for herself and not make the mistakes her mother did, Polly made straight A's in school; went to college on scholarship; earned a bachelor's degree and an MBA; and made a name and a lot of money for herself as an investment banker. She also became one of the leaders at her small church. However, due to the intense pressures of her job, Polly finally succumbed to her coworkers' urges to come to the bar with them after work. She found herself drinking more — and stronger — beverages. She tells herself she can stop drinking anytime she wants to, but in her heart she knows that her addiction is threatening the life she had so carefully built.

Sister Cringle has been greatly blessed of the Lord. But there are certain goals in her life for which she's still believing God ... a house, a reliable car, debt freedom, a Godly husband. When friends, relatives or fellow church members are blessed with these very things, she tries to be happy for them, but she is very jealous. Now Sister Cringle knows the Bible says it is a sin to be jealous and envious of others. She reminds herself of God's promises and His timing, and tries to urge herself to "be faithful over a few things." But sooner or later, resentment wells up in Sister Cringle and manifests itself in negative, critical remarks. "She better hope she don't lose her job," she says to others when Sister Brown is blessed with a new Mercedes. When Cousin Joe and his family move into a beautiful new home, Sister Cringle accuses him of thinking that he's "all that." She simply can't seem to keep from being jealous of others.

Sharita has very low self-esteem and has never recovered, psychologically or emotionally, from being sexually molested as a child. She is a Christian, but attends an old, traditional church that doesn't teach her who she is in Christ or that Jesus can heal her inner pain. Feeling disconnected from God and having no love for herself, she feels she has to have a man in order to be happy — and that in order to keep a man, she has to sleep with him. But she is anything but happy. Her "love" life consists of a rapidly-revolving door of "boyfriends" whom she hears from only at 1 or 2 in the morning, when they want to come over and have sex. Sharita would love for a Mr. Right to come along, but marriage seems more and more like a pipe dream as the Mr. Wrongs continue to show up.

These scenarios are real-life issues that are common in the Body of Christ, even more so in these last days. Saints of God, how can we live victoriously and be effective in ministry if we are in bondage? Why are Christians making choices to sin, regardless of what they know is right according to the word of God? Why are Christians allowing the enemy to trick them into thinking that the pleasures of sin will continue? The end result of sin is always destruction in some aspect of our lives. Saints of God, when we accept sin and strongholds as part of our lives, it causes a stumbling block for other Christians and may keep them from walking in the deliverance God provided for us through Jesus Christ: **"Then let us no more criticize and blame and pass**

judgment on one another, but rather decide and endeavor never to put a stumbling block or an obstacle or a hindrance in the way of a brother (Romans 14:13, AMP). If I had continued to allow strongholds to dominate my thinking, I would have become a stumbling block to others.

Strongholds caused me to have inner turmoil because of continual conflict between my soul and spirit. I knew in my heart what was right, but strongholds in my mind prevented me from obeying God's Word. It was very uncomfortable to know the truth and willingly disobey God. I was like the Apostle Paul in Romans 7:23: **"But I see another law in my members, warring against the law of my mind, and bringing me into captivity to the law of sin which is in my members"** (King James Version). Strongholds in my mind had me in bondage. I would end up obeying my flesh (soul and body) instead of my born-again spirit.

God's predestined plan for mankind is freedom from sin ... by grace, through faith in Jesus Christ. God desires for us to be free to love and obey Him. In the third chapter of Genesis, Adam and Eve disobeyed God and relinquished the freedom God had provided for them in the Garden of Eden. They allowed Satan's lies to steal their freedom, peace, and joy. Today, many Christians are in a similar state. They knowingly or unknowingly make the choice to disobey God in their thought life and lifestyles. Their choices place them in bondage, rather than the freedom they would enjoy if they would only choose to obey God's commandments.

In this book I will share my personal struggles with negative thinking, worry, vanity, jealousy, low self-esteem and obesity. God, through the power of His Word and the Holy Spirit, helped me conquer these strongholds in my life. It is essential that Christians make the choice to conquer strongholds; this will then allow the power of the Holy Spirit to be fully manifested in their lives. God desires that Christians walk in the freedom that Jesus Christ paid the price for us to have. In Galatians 5:1, the Bible admonishes us to **"stand fast therefore in the liberty wherewith Christ hath made us free, and be not entangled again with the yoke of bondage"** (KJV).

It is my prayer that this book helps Christians conquer strongholds and become the spiritually empowered people God created them to be, renewing their minds with the Word of God and making God their only stronghold.

I   Understanding Strongholds

CHAPTER 1
What Are Strongholds?

In the Old Testament, strongholds referred to fortified places in the desert or wilderness where people could hide and be protected from their enemies. This was the case with David when he was running from Saul who was trying to kill him. First Samuel 23:14 reveals that **"David stayed in the wilderness in the strongholds, and remained in the hill country in the wilderness of Ziph. And Saul sought him every day, but God did not deliver him into his hand"** (New American Standard Bible). These strongholds were high and difficult for the enemy to penetrate. Likewise, strongholds in our lives seek to rule and dominate our thought patterns and actions ... and elevate themselves above the knowledge of God.

Strongholds are habitual thought patterns, behaviors, beliefs and lifestyles that are against the will and nature of God. In the Greek translation of Biblical words, strongholds are referred to as fortresses and prisons. In one of his teachings — "Three O' Clock in the Morning: Tapping into the Spirit World" — minister and televangelist Perry Stone describes fortresses as built-up and fortified walls. Fortresses are designed to keep anything or anyone from getting inside an area. Stone describes prisons as walls that keep people or things from getting out of an area. So, using these descriptions, we can say that people dealing with spiritual strongholds have "walls" in their minds that are similar to the literal walls of fortresses and prisons. The truth of God's Word is prevented from *pen-*

etrating the mind and heart ... and sinful, ungodly thought patterns are prevented from *escaping*.

Fortresses can be compared to the high walls that Satan forms in the minds of people to keep them from living righteously. Strongholds influence a person's life in negative ways, resulting in mental, emotional, physical or spiritual pain. A person can be in denial for many years about the strongholds in his life. He may have very little desire to change because it makes him too uncomfortable to face the truth about himself. In addition, strongholds in a person's life may not be visible to others who interact with him on a daily basis. When a person is "born again," he has a brand-new *spirit*, not a brand-new mind. His mind and thinking are exactly the same as they were before he was saved. This frustrates some new Christians because they do not understand why they keep sinning. What they don't realize is that *a renewing of the mind must take place* to conquer habitual sins and strongholds. We must learn **how,** as Paul says to **"LET this mind be in you, which was also in Christ Jesus"** (Philippians 2:5, King James Version). Let means to **"allow."** We allow the mind of Christ (His word) to **dominate** our thought patterns. When I was struggling with strongholds, it was very difficult for me to concentrate on God's word and "allow" it to dominate my mind. My flesh wanted to think thoughts that were fearful, vain or jealous.

The Holy Spirit gave me a visual example of a stronghold in a person's life. Let's say that a person decides to wear a white shirt with slacks to work one day. Most likely, within a few hours the white shirt will be stained with coffee, ink or food; these stains will be visible to this person, possibly others. If this person had chosen to wear a black shirt, the stains may not be visible, but they would still be on the shirt. The stains can **only** be removed with a particular cleaning agent; however, the individual may try various other agents ... with no success. Frequently, people will try to do the same thing with strongholds in their lives. They try all types of measures to get rid of a sinful habit — everything except destroying that habit with the truth of God's Word. Since strongholds can be hidden (not visible to others), we can become comfortable with our sinful thoughts and habits and minimize their effect on our lives and the lives of others. We may say to ourselves, "Since no one knows or sees my problem, why change?" Well, God knows! And this should prompt us to have a desire to be delivered of anything that blocks our fellowship with Him.

To delve deeper into the subject of strongholds, let's examine some definitions related to the word "strongholds." In *Vine's Complete Expository Dictionary of Old and New Testament Words*, the Greek word "ochuroma" means "a stronghold fortress." The word "fortress" is defined in *Merriam-Webster's Online Thesaurus* as "a structure or place where one can resist an attack." *Webster's II New Riverside Desk Dictionary* defines the word "strong" as "difficult to break; intense, persuasive or forceful." In the same reference, the word "hold" refers to "being held or restrained; to maintain a grasp or grip." These definitions clearly show that strongholds in a person's life are powerful, deep-rooted and difficult to tear down. The person is "fixed" in his thinking about a particular subject, regardless of hearing or knowing what God's Word says about the subject.

I have known people who had beliefs that were totally against the Word of God. Some people thought they were better than other races of people. Some believed there was nothing wrong with committing fornication or having several children out of wedlock to receive money from the government. The enemy (Satan) has a foothold in the lives of people who have such beliefs. These belief systems are, most certainly, mental strongholds.

With any type of stronghold, Satan's strategy is to occupy a place in the person's mind to influence that person's thoughts and behavior. Strongholds have a strong grip on the mind and flesh, and they resist the truth of God's Word. But I want you to know that strongholds can be torn down and destroyed with God's Word — if we each make the decision to walk in the deliverance that God has already provided for us. Praise God!!!

As you continue reading this book, remember that strongholds are **habitual thought patterns, behaviors, beliefs and lifestyles that are against the will and nature of God.** Some examples of strongholds are as follows:

Negative thinking and worry
Fear
Envy and jealousy
Rage
Hatred
Low self-esteem

Comparing yourself to others
Vain thinking
Addictions
Unforgiveness
Pornography
Fornication
Adultery
Womanizing
Lust
Homosexuality
Idolatry
Prejudice

After reading this list, you may be concerned about having strongholds in your life. Fellow Christians, there is no condemnation to those who are in Christ Jesus (Romans 8:1, King James Version). So we should not allow the enemy to make us feel condemned. God loves us more than we will ever know. He sent his son Jesus to the earth to **save** us, **not to condemn us**. John 3:16-17 tells us, **"for God so loved the world, that He gave His only begotten Son, that whosoever believeth in Him should not perish, but have everlasting life. For God sent not His Son into the world to condemn the world; but that the world through Him might be saved"** (KJV). This verse reveals the love of God, who has provided deliverance from sin and death ... now, and throughout eternity. Saints of God, our heavenly Father wants us to enjoy the benefits of salvation! One of those benefits is total deliverance in all areas of our lives — if we choose to renew our minds and obey God's commandments.

For deliverance to be manifested in the natural, you must first admit to having strongholds in your life. You must then make a conscious decision to permanently destroy the strongholds with the **application** of God's Word. If we refuse to do this as Christians, strongholds will take up residence in our minds and keep us in bondage. In other words, we will be controlled by sinful habits and thinking patterns, instead of the Holy Spirit. James 4:7-8 explains how to manifest deliverance in the natural when tempted to sin: **"Submit yourselves therefore to God. Resist the devil, and he will flee from you. Draw nigh to God and He will draw**

nigh to you. Cleanse your hands, ye sinners: and purify your hearts, ye double minded" (KJV).

Submitting ourselves to the will of God means being set apart for God in spirit, soul (mind, will and emotions), and body. The Holy Spirit will empower us to resist temptations from the enemy or our own flesh when we are totally **"submitted."** Total submission allows the soul to agree with the "born-again spirit", which always wants to do what is pleasing to God. When such an agreement occurs, the power of God helps us cast down ungodly thoughts before they lead to committing sin. James 4:8 reveals that a person who has one or more strongholds is struggling with his old sinful nature. This means that some Christians need to gain understanding about their new nature (born-again spirit) and old sin nature that died with Christ when they accepted Him as Lord and Savior. Obeying our old sin nature is like trying to resurrect something that is dead.

In a study guide to his book *Grace: the Power of the Gospel*, televangelist Andrew Womack states that "you might experience some of the same emotions that you had before you were born again, but the truth is that you are dead to that sin. ... It's just an unrenewed mind that keeps these thoughts coming." (p.114). The major problem is the "unrenewed mind," not the sin. Jesus, in the flesh and on the cross, crucified sin. Now we must renew our minds to the **truth** that we are **dead to sin** and alive in Christ Jesus.

It requires daily renewing of the mind to tear down the lies and thought patterns that may have taken up residence there. The word **renewing,** in *Vine's Complete Expository Dictionary*, is *"anakainoo"* in Greek. It means **"to make new"** — as in to make new the sinful nature of **"the old mind."** For the Christian, this involves actively seeking to learn more about Christ to be like Him. The Bible says in Colossians 3:10 to **"Put on your new nature, and be renewed as you learn to know your Creator and become like Him"** (New Living Translation). God is letting us know that we must work with the Holy Spirit in developing our new nature to display the character of Christ.

CHAPTER 2
The Origin of Strongholds

Strongholds originated from Satan. He was the first created being who rebelled against God and refused to obey Him.

Let's examine the development of <u>Satan's</u> stronghold as explained in Isaiah 14:12-15 (KJV):

> **"How art thou fallen from heaven, O Lucifer, son of the morning! How art thou cut down to the ground, which didst weaken the nations! For thou hast said in thine heart, I will ascend into the heaven, I will exalt my throne above the stars of God: I will sit also upon the mount of the congregation, in the sides of the north: I will ascend above the heights of the clouds; I will be like the Most High. Yet thou shalt be brought down to hell, to the sides of the pit."**

Look at how many times Satan said the word "I." He wanted to be like the Almighty God, and receive the glory designed only for Him. Satan was obviously very **jealous** of God, as well as **prideful**. These were strongholds that led to his downfall.

The Bible describes Satan as Lucifer, a fallen angel from heaven. In heaven, he had been the worship leader, more beautiful than all the other angels. Isaiah 14:11 gives this description of Satan's defeat: **"Your pomp and the music of your harps have been brought down to Sheol; maggots are spread out as your bed beneath you and worms are your covering"** (New American Standard Bible). Satan had beauty and God-given talent, but he had no interest in using those talents to glorify God. He didn't appreciate God's purpose for him. Instead, he wanted to be *like* God — sit on a throne and be worshipped by others. Satan's strongholds and disobedience got him kicked out of heaven.

We, too, can develop strongholds in our lives when it comes to ministry work. Glorifying God and using our gifts to bless others should be the focus of all our ministry work and spiritual gifts. If we seek praise and glory for ourselves, God does not receive the glory for making us who we are.

I went through a period in my life when I wanted to receive recognition and praise from others. For instance, I was very critical of my outward appearance (hair and body size) and continually compared myself to other women. I was so concerned about what others thought about me, I would spend an hour or more on Sunday morning just trying to style my hair so that it would look perfect. This did not include the time I took to get showered and dressed! Fixated on my outward appearance, I could not see what was going on spiritually. It hurts to admit that many Sundays I literally combed my hair out. I would look in the sink after styling my hair and see numerous strands of hair in the bowl. As desperately as I wanted to have nice hair, I spent most Sunday mornings combing it out! This is just one example of how strongholds negatively impacted my life.

When I sought God about this issue, He revealed to me that I had strongholds of low self-esteem and insecurity. I had been trying to deal with these strongholds in the flesh because I had not renewed my mind to the point where I could deal with them spiritually. I had a shallow relationship with God because of habitual vain thinking. I was more concerned about what I *thought* others thought about me than what God's Word said about me.

As I went through the process of renewing my mind, the Lord showed me through His Word that I was always noticed and loved by Him no matter how I looked on the outside. He said, **"Teresia, I am always looking at you and thinking about you."** I had mixed feelings when He said this to me, but the Word of God in Psalm 40:5 calmed my fears: **"Many, O Lord my God, are thy wonderful works which thou hast done, and thy thoughts which are to us-ward: they cannot be reckoned up in order unto thee: if I would declare and speak of them, they are more than can be numbered"** (KJV). You see, God has good plans for our lives and He is always thinking about us. Look what Psalm 139:2 says! **"You** know when I sit down or stand up. You know my thoughts even when I'm far away"** (NLT).

When I realized that God was always thinking about me and knew my thoughts, I began to stop seeking the attention of others. I already had the attention of the Almighty God, and He was more wonderful and lovely than anyone I could ever imagine. This love from God caused me to want to live **holy** in spirit, soul and body. In fact, this was the first time I really considered what it meant to live holy with my entire being. From that day forward, I wanted to please God in every area of my life. But, it was my responsibility to truly seek God so I would know His wonderful plans for my life.

God is concerned about every facet of our lives, but He desires that we make developing godly character a priority. Children of God, Satan's goal is to keep us bound with carnal, fleshly desires so that we will be focused on ourselves all the time. We are fighting a losing battle if we think we can completely please our flesh (the *lower, sinful* nature of man, according to *Vine's Complete Expository Dictionary*). Satan's method of influencing people is through the flesh (mind and body). He cannot influence us through our born-again spirits. Romans 7:18 (KJV) gives us a glimpse into the destructive nature of the flesh — **"For I know that in me (that is, in my flesh) dwelleth no good thing"** — as does Romans 8:8: **"So then they that are in the flesh cannot please God."** We must stop catering to the appetites of our flesh because it cannot please God and it will never be satisfied. We may *tell* ourselves that we will stop sleeping around so much, cut back on using drugs, stop overeating, etc. But if we habitually commit a sin, regardless of the frequency with which we commit it, the flesh will only want more and more. That stronghold will remain in our mind and flesh because we are harboring it and it has taken up residence. This is exactly what Satan wants so he can continue influencing our behavior and thoughts.

John 10:10 states that **"the thief cometh not, but for to steal, and to kill, and to destroy: I am come that they might have life, and that they might have it more abundantly"** (KJV). When we leave an open door for the enemy, he will come in and wreak havoc in our lives. Strongholds in our lives cause us to settle for momentary pleasures. We must each **desire** to have what God **predestined** us to have — an abundant, victorious life, now and throughout eternity.

Chapter 3
The Lie: How Strongholds Entered the Human Race

In the first chapter of Genesis, we find that everything God created was very good. **"And God saw everything that He had made, and, behold, it was very good. And the evening and the morning were the sixth day"** (Genesis 1:31, KJV). God's predestined plan for mankind was to live in perfect harmony with us in a perfect place. The Garden of Eden was absolutely perfect. Adam and Eve were living in an environment that was free of sin, sickness or disease. Nothing prevented them from being in constant fellowship with God. The only thing God told Adam NOT to do was eat from the tree of "knowledge of good and evil" (Genesis 2:17). We find out later in scripture that Eve was also aware of this instruction God gave to Adam.

The book of Genesis reveals that the serpent (Satan), who had many strongholds, was also in the Garden during this time (Genesis 3:1). The serpent is the Bible's first evil being. This proves he was the avenue by which strongholds entered the human race. Satan approached Eve and tempted her to question God's instruction to avoid eating of the tree of knowledge of good and evil. He planted a "thought" in her mind. Strongholds begin with a thought or thought pattern that disagrees with the Word of God. Satan asked this question in the latter part of Genesis 3:1: **"Did God *really* say you must not eat the fruit from any of the trees in the garden?"** (NLT). Both Adam and Eve made the mistake of allowing Satan to influence their thinking instead of taking authority over him. Their failure to immediately take authority gave Satan an opportunity to tempt Eve further by causing her to question God's authority and goodness (Genesis 3:6). Eve took her mind off God's instructions and began to **lust** after the beautiful fruit on the tree of knowledge of good and evil.

The situation that occurred between Eve and Satan describes the way strongholds operate in a person's life. For example, Satan was successful in causing Eve to elevate her desire to taste the fruit above God's instructions. That is his tactic — to appeal to the flesh and the outward appearance so that his victim will ignore the born-again spirit that desires to be obedient. Strongholds seek to dominate a person's mind, will and emotions. Eve made the choice to eat the forbidden fruit and her decision convinced Adam to eat it too. Therefore, strongholds fully entered the human race through one man (Adam), because he disobeyed God.

Ever since the incident in the Garden of Eden, mankind in general has struggled with such strongholds as anger, lust, jealousy, fornication, adultery, addictions and fear. Christians who have strongholds in their lives make similar choices to sin, regardless of God's instructions in the Bible. They may know what God's Word says about hatred or committing adultery, but they make the choice to continue engaging in these sinful acts. In many instances, the lives of Christians and non-Christians alike are destroyed because of strongholds in their lives.

In Genesis 4:3-7 (NLT), we see a description of Cain's strongholds of jealousy and anger:

> **"When it was time for the harvest, Cain presented some of his crops as a gift to the Lord. Abel also brought a gift — the best of the firstborn lambs from his flock. The Lord accepted Abel and his gift, but He did not accept Cain and his gift. This made Cain very angry, and he looked dejected. Why are you so angry? The Lord asked Cain. Why do you look so dejected? You will be accepted if you do what is right. But if you refuse to do what is right, then watch out.! Sin is crouching at the door, eager to control you. But you must subdue it and be its master."**

It is interesting to note in this scripture that the Lord not only accepted Abel's gift, but He accepted **Abel**. Abel gave the **"best"** of his firstborn lambs, while Cain gave **"some"** of his crops. Abel gave his best because he believed God and wanted to worship Him with his offering.

This was not the case with Cain. Let's examine three points about Cain that reveal he had strongholds in his mind:

1. **Cain did not take the opportunity God gave him to do what was right so that his gift would be accepted.** Cain refused to obey God. He elevated his will above God's will. Christians with strongholds in their thinking do the same thing when they decide to follow their own standards of right and wrong instead of obeying God's Word. Cain set his own standards when he chose his gift for God. As Christians, we do the very same thing when we decide our own standard of what is "right." For example, we may decide to give offerings instead of tithing, or we may refuse to forgive when we know God's Word says that walking in love includes forgiving others who have hurt us.

2. **Cain remained angry after being confronted by God.** Cain allowed his sinful thoughts and feelings to become so intense that he made the choice to kill his brother. There is a lesson we can learn from this story. It is crucial that we deal with thoughts and behaviors that are displeasing to God, because they will only lead to destruction in our lives. Ungodly thoughts provide an open door for Satan to tempt or attack us. The Bible says that Satan (the instigator of strongholds) comes to steal, kill and destroy (John 10:10).

3. **God warned Cain that his sinful behavior would control him if he didn't take authority over the enemy influencing him.** Cain killed his brother Abel because, contrary to God's request, he refused to deal with his anger. Many of us may have allowed our angry feelings to get out of control, resulting in disastrous situations. I know from personal experience that we do not have to continue living this way. We can **refuse** to hold on to sinful thoughts and behaviors. We can confess them to Christ. The Holy Spirit is always available to help us calm down and make godly decisions when faced with challenges.

II Where Strongholds Reside

CHAPTER 4
Our Thought Life: A Seed is Planted

The previous chapter described how Adam and Eve allowed Satan to influence their thinking ... which led to spiritual death. Before we proceed further in this chapter, let's examine the meaning of the word "thought." *Webster's Dictionary* defines "thought" **as "the act, process or power of thinking, a product of thinking, idea, body of ideas, and attentive consideration."** Thoughts require thinking, deliberation and meditation. The first mistake Adam and Eve made was to listen to Satan. They gave Satan their full attention and **meditated** on his words. They relinquished their God-given authority over the enemy and allowed his words and ideas to elevate above God's Word in their hearts. Adam and Eve allowed their flesh to lead them instead of God. They believed Satan's explanation as to why they were told not to eat from the tree of knowledge of good and evil. Eve's meditation on the enemy's words caused her to lust after the fruit and desire to eat it.

Now we can see the pattern that led to the ungodly thoughts being planted in Eve's mind. First of all, Eve listened to the enemy and gave him her full attention, and then she allowed the enemy's lies to be elevated above God's Word. At this point Eve was allowing the enemy's seed to be planted firmly in her mind. According to the Random House Webster's College Thesaurus the word "seed" refers to the beginning of a kernel or germ that is sown. When the seed (false thought, or germ) was planted,

Eve's flesh took over and she began to look at the fruit with lustful eyes. She began to *imagine what Satan said would happen* if she ate the forbidden fruit. Her lust led to disobedience (the eating of the fruit). Genesis 3:6 states: **"And when the woman saw that the tree was good for food, and that it was pleasant to the eyes, and a tree to be desired to make one wise, she took of the fruit thereof, and did eat, and gave also unto her husband with her; and he did eat"** (KJV). How could this happen when Adam and Eve had been continually abiding with God in the garden? How did Adam and Eve make this choice after living in a perfect environment where all their needs were met?

Having a perfect environment (home, work, ministry, body, and relationships) cannot replace or compare with what we have as children of the Most High God. Satan will always try to make us think there is something better than what God has already provided for us through Jesus Christ.

Our daughter Amanda, who is a young adult, shared with me a revelation she received from the Holy Spirit about Satan's lies. She stated that Adam and Eve believed a lie from Satan because they thought eating the forbidden fruit would make life more pleasurable. "This is the same lie people [young and old] believe today," she pointed out. Satan makes them think that sin is more pleasurable than living holy for God, then fools them into believing that the pleasures they derive from sinning will never end. Satan also wants people to believe they will not experience the consequences of sin. (A sad fact is that even some Christians view the Christian life as boring. It is the exact opposite. The Christian life is the most exciting life a person can ever live! If you are young in Christ, just continue growing in Him and watch Him do marvelous things through you.)

Amanda went on to say that the main reason some Christians do not have a passion for the things of God is because they continue to believe the lie that originated in the Garden of Eden. Satan's trick is to make people think he has something more pleasurable and valuable than God. And that is so untrue! **There is no way that Satan, who was kicked out of heaven and later defeated by Jesus Christ, can give us anything that is better than God's grace.** Satan is a liar and a deceiver. Nothing about him is good. Therefore anything he offers us (money, fame, power, sex, drugs,) will eventually destroy us. Do you remember the scenario about

Pastor Glover in the Introduction of this book? It was a good example of someone thinking that the pleasures of sin will continue.

As mentioned earlier, Adam and Eve were in continual fellowship with God … yet they felt they were missing out on something better. They believed "the lie" and meditated on the enemy's words. Consequently, Adam and Eve relinquished their God-given authority over Satan. They had the opportunity and ability to immediately rebuke Satan when he approached them, but they did not do it. Second Corinthians 10:4-5 tells us that **"the weapons of our warfare are not carnal, but mighty through God to the pulling down of strongholds; casting down imaginations, and every high thing that exalteth itself against the knowledge of God, and bringing into captivity every thought to the obedience of Christ"** (KJV). Adam and Eve should have cast down the imaginations about the fruit — imaginations that had elevated themselves above their knowledge of God. God wanted them to immediately expose those thoughts to Him so they could remain in obedience.

There are two words in 2nd Corinthians 10:5 that need to be emphasized. They are **"imaginations" and "thoughts."** *Vine's Complete Expository Dictionary* states that imagination is called "logismos" in the Greek translation. Logismos refers to "reasoning, a thought of evil intent." According to this scriptural reference, we as Christians are to cast down imaginations based on our consciences. Therefore, we must **recognize,** through our consciences or hearts, thought patterns that **disagree** with the Word of God **before** they become imaginations in our minds. In other words, we practice recognizing and casting down sinful thoughts before we imagine **committing** the sin.

Dr. Caroline Leaf shares some interesting research findings about thoughts in her book *Who Switched off My Brain: Controlling Toxic Thoughts and Emotions.* Scientists have been able to prove through research that 87 percent of illnesses are directly related to the thought life (p. 4). Wow! this fact floored me. This research provides the reason my health began to improve when I dealt with the strongholds of worry and negative thinking in my life. Dr. Leaf also discusses how correct or godly thought patterns can build **good strongholds** in our minds (p. 8). The opposite is also true — evil **imaginations,** or habitual ungodly thoughts patterns, can build **bad strongholds** in our minds.

God spoke to Jeremiah about the imaginations in the hearts of the people of Judah: **"This evil people, which refuse to hear my words, which walk in the imagination of their heart, and walk after other gods, to serve them, and to worship them, shall even be as this girdle, which is good for nothing"** (Jeremiah 13:10, KJV). Fleshly, sinful thoughts led the people of Judah to have images in their minds of other gods. Their flesh acted upon these images and they chose to worship and serve idol gods. If a person imagines or visualizes something long enough, his flesh will eventually desire that thing, food or person. For instance, if I think about eating a barbecue sandwich all day long, I will develop a strong desire to buy one within the next few days. This is because I meditated on the thought and my flesh began to crave the sandwich.

Christians who want to be delivered from sinful habits must avoid *meditating* on them. Instead, they should meditate on scriptures that describe their new nature, which is born of God, righteous, holy, eternal and victorious. Joshua 1:8 states, **"This book of the law shall not depart out of thy mouth, but thou shalt meditate therein day and night, that thou mayest observe to do according to all that is written therein: for then thou shalt make thy way prosperous, and then thou shalt have good success"** (KJV). Meditating on God's Word gives us the desire to live righteous lives instead of unrighteous lives. Having conquered strongholds in my life, I am still sometimes tempted to do or say something that would not be Christlike. When I immediately meditate on the Word of God, the temptation leaves me. God promises us that if we meditate on His Word day and night, we will be successful. Think for a moment about the people in the Bible who chose to live by the Word of God when faced with temptations (Abraham, Noah, Job, David, Joseph, Esther, Jesus, Paul and many others) and even faced adversity and ridicule when making the choice to live righteously. Consequently, God was glorified and they were very successful in fulfilling His call on their lives.

Saints of God, the same thing applies to us today. When we make the choice to live righteously, God is glorified and His blessings will be manifested in our lives even in the face of adversity.

CHAPTER 5
The Development of Strongholds in the Mind

Strongholds may develop in a person's life for many reasons. One of the main reasons Christians have strongholds is because their minds have not been renewed with the Word of God.

Before we go further, let's examine the word "mind." This will give you a better understanding when it is mentioned in the upcoming chapters. The word "mind" refers **to "the part of a human being that governs thought, perception, feeling, will, memory and imagination"** (*Webster's II New Riverside Desk Dictionary*). In *Vine's Complete Expository Dictionary*, the word *"mind"* as a noun refers to perception, understanding, judging and determining. In the New Testament, the word "mind" refers to **"the faculty of knowing, the seat of understanding."** The mind also includes our intellect. When we combine these definitions, we see that the mind is the place where thoughts, ability to perceive, choices and imaginations reflect what we *know and understand*. If our thoughts, choices and imaginations are habitually ungodly in certain areas and we have problems perceiving this about ourselves, then we really do not *know and understand* God's Word. Genesis 6:5 says, **"And God saw that the wickedness of man was great in the earth, and that every *imagination of the thoughts* of his heart was only evil continually"** (KJV). The people in Noah's day refused to heed the Word of God spoken through Noah. If they had known and understood God, they would have listened to Noah and stopped committing evil deeds.

In my earlier years, I really did not know and understand the Word of God on a level that enabled me to conquer strongholds. I kept struggling in my mind and flesh, when I needed to be transformed by the renewing of my mind so my soul *(mind, will and emotions)* could agree with my born-again spirit. My born-again spirit wanted to do what was right in God's Word, but strongholds caused me to struggle in my mind. Many times I made the wrong choice and pleased my flesh instead of God.

Being born again does not mean that a person's thought patterns will instantly change to agree with God's Word. God instructs us as Christians to transform our minds in Romans 12:2: **"And be not conformed to this world: but be ye transformed by the renewing of your mind, that ye may prove what is that good, and acceptable, and perfect, will of God"** (KJV). The Greek word "transform" in *Vine's Complete Expository Dictionary* is translated as "metamorpoo" *(changed in form)*. The English version of the word "metamorphosis" is defined as supernatural transformation, "a marked alteration in appearance, condition, character and function" (*Webster's II New Riverside Dictionary*). Saints of God, when our minds have been transformed there will be a drastic change in speech, conduct, lifestyle and behavior for each of us. God has delivered us from darkness and translated us into the Kingdom of his dear Son (Colossians 1:13)., but we must do our part in the total transformation. God has given us His Word, Jesus, and the Holy Spirit to make sure we have access to everything we need to conquer strongholds. It is our responsibility to deal with the strongholds by using everything God has provided. The Bible says that the Holy Spirit is our teacher, helper, encourager and comforter (John 14:16-17)

In addition to unrenewed Christian minds, breeding grounds for strongholds include painful childhood experiences; growing up in a home with ungodly values; trauma; demonic oppression; carnal lifestyles; and a simple lack of knowledge about God's word.

Let's look at the first of these. Some people grew up in families in which there was physical, sexual or emotional abuse. These painful experiences led to thought patterns that influenced how they related to others as adults. Some people really do not know what it is like to grow up in a so-called normal family. Their family situations have always been stressful and chaotic. If any situation occurs that reminds them of their painful experiences as children, they may respond negatively to try to protect themselves. Mental strongholds may affect how they relate to people in society in general.

Regardless of the reason for strongholds, God gave us the Holy Spirit and His Word to teach us how to conquer any painful experience in life. Some Christians have learned how to be good fathers, mothers and friends by studying the Word of God and applying its principles in their lives. I have heard testimonies of Christian men who stated they did not have a father to teach them how to be godly men. They learned how, these men said, by applying biblical principles in their lives and spending time with godly men in their church or community.

Now let's look at the second of these breeding grounds for strongholds. I remember talking to a young man who was in substance-abuse treatment. He described to me what it was like to be raised in a family with ungodly values. He stated that the reason he was unfaithful to his wife was because all the men in his family were unfaithful to their wives. This young man had learned wrong values from the other men in his family. He thought it was acceptable for men to cheat on their wives, although he knew in his heart this was wrong. Thank God that this man learned, while being treated for his addiction, that his value system was wrong and that he had the power to change it! I do not know whether he was a Christian, but I do know that his mind needed to be renewed to understand God's beautiful plan for marriage. What if this young man had known *(recognized, understood, realized)* that God wanted him to love his wife as Christ loved the church and gave His life for it (Ephesians 5:25) What would his marriage be like had he known that husbands and wives are to submit to one another in fear (reverence) for God (Ephesians 5:21) Scores of Christians may have grown up in environments in which they learned wrong values that impacted their lives in negative ways. It can be very difficult to change values that we grew up believing were normal or acceptable. In some instances, negative consequences may cause some people to change their values. But the best way to change wrong values is to conquer strongholds by renewing our minds with the Word of God.

The woman described in the fourth chapter of John is a prime example of a woman who had strongholds in her life. First of all, she was born a Samaritan. The Samaritans were a mixed race of Jews, hated by pure Jews. The Samaritan woman knew early on that the Jews thought they were superior to the Samaritans. Early in the Samaritan woman's childhood, she most likely experienced prejudice and painful experiences that caused her to have low self-esteem. I believe that a stronghold of low self-esteem influenced the decisions she made throughout her life until she met Jesus. This stronghold caused the Samaritan woman to make ungodly choices in an attempt to prove her self-worth.

The scriptures tell us that the Samaritan woman was promiscuous and always had a man in her life ... whether she was married to him or not. She had a stronghold of committing fornication: **"Jesus said unto her, Go, call thy husband, and come hither. The woman answered and said, I have no husband. Jesus said unto her, Thou hast well said, I have no husband: For thou hast had five husbands: and he whom thou now hast is not thy husband: in that saidst thou truly"** (John 4: 16-18, KJV).

Initially, the Samaritan woman could not receive truth from Jesus when He was speaking to her. He had to get up close and personal to get her attention. When her stronghold was exposed by Jesus, whom she did not know, she perceived that Jesus was Christ the Messiah. John 4:25-26 (KJV) reveals her perception of Him as the Christ: **"The woman saith unto him, I know that Messias cometh, which is called Christ: when He is come, He will tell us all things. Jesus saith unto her, I that speak unto thee am He."** The Samaritan woman believed Him. Isn't it wonderful to see that Jesus showed up to deliver the Samaritan woman from her strongholds — not to condemn her?

The Samaritan woman's desire for the *"living water"* from Jesus set her free from bondage to strongholds. She had spent many years trying to meet the needs of her flesh and was never satisfied. That day, the Samaritan woman received satisfaction on a level that she had never experienced before. This leads me to ask, "What do some Christians really desire?" When we truly **desire** and seek God, He heals and delivers us. This is a key to deliverance from strongholds, a key I will discuss later.

After her deliverance, the Samaritan woman was free to allow the power of God to flow through her. She left her water pot and went to the city to talk to men who knew her previous lifestyle. In other words, she went back to the "hood." Old things in her life had passed away and she was a brand-new creature in Christ. This woman had the power of God in her to preach her first sermon. She said, **"Come, see a man, which told me all things that ever I did: is not this the Christ?** (John 4:29, KJV). The passage goes on to say that the men left the city and came to see Jesus. They knew that a miracle had taken place in the woman's life that day.

Many of the Samaritans accepted Jesus because of the Samaritan woman's testimony and changed life. This is what can happen when a person is delivered from strongholds. He is free to be who God created him to be. If I had not made the choice to renew my mind, I would not be free to write this book so that others could be delivered from strongholds.

By now, you may have identified a stronghold in your life that you need to conquer. Just know that the power of God is available to you right now. All you need to do is seek Him with your whole heart and begin to renew your mind with the word of God.

CHAPTER 6
The Mind: The Stronghold's Battleground

To understand how the mind becomes the battleground for strongholds, we need to review how God created us. First of all, we are **spirit** beings. The spirit is the temple of God, where the Holy Spirit dwells. Nothing can change this if we are truly born again. We each have a soul (mind, will and emotions) and we each live in a physical body. First Thessalonians 5:23 states: **"And the very God of peace sanctify you wholly; and I pray God your whole spirit and soul and body be preserved blameless unto the coming of our Lord Jesus Christ"** (KJV). God desires of each of us that our entire being be dedicated to Him. Our spirits were made brand-new when we accepted Jesus as our Lord and Savior. Therefore, our spirits, through the power of the Holy Spirit, should control our souls and bodies. The **opposite** occurs when we have strongholds in our lives. The flesh (body and soul) teams up and goes against what we know is right in our hearts (spirits). The body and soul represents the flesh and lower nature. The "flesh" is the part of our being that lacks the will and nature of God. The flesh is against God and it is weak. The Bible says, **"Watch and pray, that ye enter not into temptation: the spirit indeed is willing, but the flesh is weak** (Matthew 26:41, KJV). The flesh is never satisfied. The flesh desires more and more pleasure, regardless of the danger or consequences. However, when we daily renew our minds, our souls can agree with our born-again spirits. The body has to follow whatever choice is made with the mind.

Now that we have laid some groundwork, let's look at the battle that occurs in the mind of someone who has strongholds in his life. The mind ("the faculty of knowing, the seat of understanding," according to *Vine's Complete Expository Dictionary*) is the battleground on which people struggle with strongholds.

To give you a clearer picture of this battle, I want to describe my previous bondage to sweets, specifically cookies. My closest friends and family members know that I find cookies irresistible. I have jokingly called myself the "cookie monster." Cookies made me change into another person when I saw them. I have stood in the cookie aisle at the grocery store for 15 minutes, looking at all the cookies and imagining their taste. I would hold a box of cookies for a while and put it back down. Then I'd pick up another box of cookies. I'd do the same thing over and over again. I was having a battle in my mind because my spirit was telling me that it was harmful to my health to eat so many sweets. But my flesh craved cookies, and had me rationalizing why I could still eat them. You see, buying a box of cookies meant that I would eat the cookies until they were all gone and usually gain 2-3 pounds. I didn't have the discipline to eat one or two cookies. I would eat 10 to 15 within just a few minutes.

For many years, I committed the sin of gluttony by eating too many cookies or other sweets. I remember eating a whole box of Girl Scout Thin Mint cookies in less than 20 minutes. I rationalized that the cookies were small and I might as well eat the whole box so I wouldn't be eating them the next day. I felt sick afterwards and I was so mad at myself for doing this. Why wouldn't I stop after eating three or four cookies? The more I ate, the more I wanted. Remember my earlier mention that the flesh is never satisfied? The addiction to cookies was a stronghold that I needed to conquer. In my mind I **knew** that it was wrong to eat excessive amounts of sweets. I also had an **understanding** of the consequences. The problem was that I had free will and I allowed my flesh to dominate.

With all strongholds, the soul is **minding** the things of the flesh and persuading the person to continue thinking and acting in a way that is against the Word of God. The person may desire to do what is right, but feels that a **"strong force"** keeps him from obeying God. This just means that the enemy has, or is trying to occupy, a place in his mind to keep him from being obedient.

God created us with free will to choose what we want in life. And we get in trouble when we are not disciplined to choose God's commandments. The enemy's tactic with any stronghold is to occupy a place in our minds so that we are continually struggling with sinful thoughts and behaviors. (I was continually struggling with eating sweets and cookies.) A person may know in his heart what is right, but the stronghold dominates and wins the battle in his mind. The Bible says, via Galatians 5:17, "**For the flesh lusteth against the Spirit, and the Spirit against the flesh: and these are contrary the one to the other: so that ye cannot do the things that ye would**" (KJV). In the New Living Translation, the verse reads, "**The sinful nature wants to do evil, which is just the opposite of what the spirit wants. And the Spirit gives us desires that are the opposite of what the sinful nature desires. These two forces are constantly fighting each other, so you are not free to carry out your good intentions.**"

When I went grocery shopping I had every intention of avoiding the cookie aisle, but my flesh wanted to do the complete opposite. Since I had not conquered the stronghold of eating excessive amounts of sweets, I could not carry out my plan of not buying cookies. When I embraced the truth of God's Word about taking care of His temple, I was able to avoid going to the cookie aisle. I am not saying that I never eat cookies or sweets. Occasionally, I will eat too many sweets, but I am able to get back on track with what I know is right. I rarely buy large bags of cookies at the grocery store anymore. Many times I will purposely avoid walking down the "cookie aisle." I am learning to yield to the Holy Spirit, and He empowers me to have self-control.

CHAPTER 7
The Flesh: The Stronghold's Attachment and Root

An essential factor in conquering strongholds is getting to the **root** of the stronghold. The root is the basis for the stronghold and must be dealt with spiritually. Neglecting the root is like putting a Band-Aid over an infected sore without treating the bacteria that caused the infection. The infection remains and actually gets worse because its source was not treated.

Several years ago, my husband and I won a "yard makeover" in a local television contest. We received new grass, flowers, trees, a hot tub and a riding lawnmower. We loved our new yard, but we had to work very hard to keep grass and weeds from growing around our beautiful new flowers and trees. During the spring and summer, we tried to keep up a schedule of working in the yard several times a week. If we went a couple of weeks without working in the yard, the weeds would grow up and develop a root system under the flowers. It was very difficult to remove these weeds once a root system had developed. So it is with strongholds. If we do not deal with the roots to the strongholds in our lives, the strongholds will eventually resurface.

In today's society, we hear of several instances in which ministers or ministry leaders are caught committing sinful actions such as affairs, sexual encounters and theft. These are often people who have had successful ministries for many years. I believe these individuals did not effectively conquer the strongholds in their lives — more specifically, they did not destroy the roots to their strongholds. A minister may have gone years without committing the sin in which he was caught ... but because the root was still there, the stronghold resurfaced.

The word "root" in Greek as a noun refers to the "cause, origin, or source" of something (*Vine's Complete Expository Dictionary*). It is important that we each seek the Holy Spirit's guidance in determining the root of any stronghold we desire to conquer.

Let's examine some scriptures that refer to the "root" and see how we can apply this knowledge to conquering strongholds. In Mark 11:13-14, Jesus, who was walking with his disciples, was hungry. The group saw a fig tree. Jesus desired its fruit. But the tree, although it appeared healthy, bore no figs. Jesus spoke to the tree and stated, **"No man eat fruit of thee hereafter forever"** (Mark 11:14, KJV). The next morning, Jesus and Peter were walking and passed by the tree again. The tree had completely withered away at the **roots** (its origin or source). Peter reminded Jesus that He had previously cursed the fig tree: **"And in the morning, as they passed by, they saw the fig tree dried up from the roots. And Peter calling to remembrance saith unto him, Master, behold, the fig tree which thou cursedst is withered away"** (Mark 11:20-21).

Look at the supernatural power of God to destroy the roots and leaves of a large fig tree in less than 24 hours! Jesus made sure the fig tree would **never again produce** leaves or fruit. He spoke to the fig tree's origin, or root, to destroy it. We can do the same thing with any strongholds in our lives, because God's power is within us. If a person wants never to commit a certain sin again, he must speak to the root that leads to the sin by lining up his thinking with the Word of God. In essence, we agree to live the way God says we should live. So why are some Christians reluctant to do this when there is a habitual sin in their lives? I believe it is because we don't really understand that there are underlying roots to most strongholds. Dealing with our roots means we must deal with things that may be uncomfortable to our flesh. In addition, our flesh does not want to give up sinful pleasures. Saints, if we don't deal with the roots to our strongholds, Satan has us right where he wants us (hiding and covering up sin)!

I remember walking one day and talking with the Lord about a stronghold with which I had struggled for many years. I constantly compared myself to other people, especially their looks and their possessions. This was really beginning to disturb me. I wanted to get to the source (root) of this stronghold, so I asked the Lord why I thought this way. He clearly impressed it upon my spirit that I had developed this ungodly thought pattern because of lingering low self-esteem from being an overweight child. Throughout my childhood I was compared to my younger sisters, who were slim. When we visited relatives, I was frequently made aware of my size compared to my sisters' sizes. My relatives did not do this to intentionally hurt me, but their comments always made me feel self-conscious about my size. I became overly concerned about my weight, hair and appearance. These thoughts and feelings of low self-esteem continued to affect me as an adult ... and always comparing myself to others was a byproduct of the stronghold! It wasn't until I made a decision to conquer strongholds in my life that I associated some of them with these past experiences.

It was so liberating to understand how the stronghold of comparison had developed. After the revelation from the Lord regarding its origin, I made a conscious decision to work on improving my physical and mental health. I stopped focusing on others and began focusing on what God wanted to do through me. I started meditating more on the Word, began walking and changed my eating habits. This freedom from bondage caused me to have more joy in my relationship with the Lord. Psalm 16:11 states, **"You will show me the way of life, granting me the joy of your presence and the pleasures of living with you forever"** (NLT). As I sought God, He showed me how to live a life that was pleasing to Him.

Among the positive results was a transformation of mind and body ... I lost more than 40 pounds! I needed to conquer the obesity stronghold that had not only gripped me, but which had been in my family for many years. Several of my family members have died early — in their 20s, 40s, 50s and 60s — because of obesity, which resulted in heart disease and diabetes. I refused to allow this stronghold to continue in my life. I wanted to set a good example for my children and other loved ones so they, too, would desire to improve their physical and mental health.

I would advise all Christians to ask the Holy Spirit to show them the truth about themselves by revealing the roots to all their strongholds. The Bible says that the Holy Spirit is the "spirit of truth" in John 14:17: **"Even the Spirit of truth; whom the world cannot receive, because it seeth Him not, neither knoweth Him: but ye know Him; for He dwelleth with you, and shall be in you"** (KJV). Saints of God, the Spirit of Truth lives within us. We need to **seek His wisdom and listen.**

The origin of a stronghold is the method Satan uses to keep us operating out of our flesh. In other words, when the **"root"** of a stronghold is not destroyed, there's an open door for Satan to influence our thoughts and behaviors. Once we know our strongholds' origins, we can effectively destroy those strongholds with the truth of God's Word, along with prayer and obedience. A clear understanding of the root of a stronghold helps each of us see its attachment to our flesh. The flesh is that part of our being that lacks the nature and will of God. The only part of us made new when we were born again was our spirit. The soul (mind, will and emotions) requires renewing on a daily basis so that it can agree with the born-again spirit. The body, which is part of the flesh, obeys the choice the mind makes regarding any circumstance. One of the reasons we have temptations is because the flesh has a mind of its own. It wants what it wants when it wants it!!! Romans 8:5 states **"for they that are after the flesh do mind the things of the flesh; but they that are after the Spirit the things of the Spirit"** (KJV). The New Living Translation states that **"Those who are dominated by the sinful nature think about sinful things, but those who are controlled by the Holy Spirit think about things that please the Spirit. So letting your sinful nature control your mind leads to death. But letting the Spirit control your mind leads to life and peace"** (Romans 8:5-6.) Brothers and sisters in Christ, we were each designed by God to be controlled by our born-again spirit.

Remember the Samaritan woman whose story was shared in Chapter 5? I believe that the root (origin) of her strongholds was the need to be recognized as a worthwhile human being. She experienced humiliation as a Samaritan and sought out relationships with men to meet the need of feeling worthwhile. The Samaritan woman's mind was on meeting the needs of her flesh. This was her temporary fix for the pain she experienced in her soul. The Samaritan woman's flesh craved attention and approval. Since her sinful nature dominated, her mind made the choice to commit fornication. Jesus showed up in this woman's life one day and gave her a desire to have a relationship with Him. The Samaritan woman received the love of an eternal God who came to earth to save her. *She realized how precious she was in His sight.*

You may have encountered similar issues in your life. Just like the Samaritan woman, you can receive God's love and healing. First of all, desire a close relationship with the Lord Jesus Christ. He loves you and wants your undivided attention. (Many times we cannot give God our undivided attention because our minds are focused on carnal and fleshly things. For example, our main concerns may be on pleasing others, gaining more material possessions, or satisfying our other fleshly desires. All of these things interfere with the development of a close relationship with God.)

Once you have dealt with the root to your strongholds, the Bible shows you how to take authority over fleshly desires: **"Therefore, dear brothers and sisters, you have <u>no obligation to do what your sinful nature urges you to do</u>. For if you live by its dictates, you will die. But if through the power of the Spirit you put to death the deeds of your sinful nature, you will live"** (Romans 8:12-13, NLT). Remember the scenario about Pastor Glover in the Introduction? Well, it is obvious that he never dealt with the root to his strongholds of lust and womanizing. If Pastor Glover had destroyed the root with deep soul-searching and wisdom from God, he would have immediately cast down lustful thoughts and confessed them to Christ. He may have even sought counseling before he committed those sins. He did not have to live by the dictates of his flesh. Brothers and sisters, we are not obligated to do what our flesh tells us to do. It died with Christ, and has no power or authority. The flesh is just the stronghold's root and attachment. The flesh must be crucified daily with the power and Word of God. Galatians 2:20 says, **"I am crucified with Christ: nevertheless I live; yet not I, but Christ liveth in me"** (KJV). Andrew Womack, in the study guide to his book *Grace: The Power of the Gospel*, explains this passage of scripture this way: **"Your old man died with Christ. Somehow, Jesus was able to take your sin — not your individual sins only, but your sin nature, your old man … upon Himself when He died. Now your sin nature is dead. It's gone — nonexistent"** (p. 177).

Allowing the Holy Spirit to rule and reign in our lives helps us take authority over fleshly desires. This simply means we decide to choose "life" instead of death. Deuteronomy 30:19 puts it this way: **"I call heaven and earth to record this day against you, that I have set before you life and death, blessing and cursing: therefore *choose life that both thou and thy seed may live.*"** Choosing life means conquering any stronghold that robs us of our victorious **life** in Christ. God tells us to choose life just in case we don't know what true life is.

III Identifying Strongholds in Your Life

CHAPTER 8
God's Predestined Plan

Again, I allowed strongholds to develop in my mind because of low-self esteem, jealousy and laziness in studying the Word of God. I didn't properly deal with painful experiences in my life, and I allowed negative emotions to go unchecked. I spent years comparing myself to others instead of Christ. I tried to appear as though I had it all together on the outside, but inwardly I was frequently miserable. I felt that I had very little control over my recurring negative, jealous and vain thoughts. My spirit was not disciplined to take authority over the thoughts and cast them down. So eventually I gave in to thinking, and sometimes behaving, in ways that were sinful. This made me feel ashamed and guilty because I knew that God knew my thoughts. Psalm 94:11 says that **"The Lord knoweth the thoughts of man, that they are vanity"** (KJV). God desires that our thoughts be pleasing to Him because our thoughts lead to our feelings and behavior: **"Let the words of my mouth, and the meditation of my heart, be acceptable in thy sight, O Lord, my strength, and my redeemer"** (Psalm 19:14, KJV).

A strong desire to live holy is what motivated me to identify strongholds in my life. I was also tired of thinking the same thoughts, but expecting different results. God said in His Word that we are a royal priesthood and a holy nation (1st Peter 2:9), but I didn't think I was "living" holy. I had to choose to conquer strongholds so I could live holy. Ephesians 1:4-5 states, **"According as He hath chosen us in Him before the foundation of the world, that we should be holy and without blame before Him in love: Having predestinated us into the adoption of children by Jesus Christ to himself, according to the good pleasure of his will"** (KJV). Before the foundation of the world, God predestinated, or predestined, us to live holy so we could be "set apart" for Him in spirit, soul and body.

It got to the point that I wanted to please God more than I wanted anything else. The Bible says we are to love God with our whole heart, soul and mind. I had to admit that strongholds prevented me from loving God with my whole soul (mind, will and emotions). In my heart I loved God, but my mind was sometimes preoccupied with carnal or ungodly thoughts. Let me remind you that I was attending church every Sunday while harboring strongholds in my life!

I truly believe that "living holy" should be taught and emphasized more in our churches. Many people with whom I have talked have a *vague* understanding about holiness ... not the understanding that being holy means being set apart for God in spirit, soul and body. Some African-American Christians think that living holy means being "sanctified." In what used to be known as the "sanctified church," people did not wear jewelry; the ladies wore dresses only, and wore no makeup. The focus was on the outward appearance. Christians need a better understanding of what it *really* means to live holy, and how living holy causes them to prosper. This is God's predestined plan for his children. Prosperity is about so much more than having money! Prosperity includes godly wisdom, good health, favor, resources and a family that is saved.

Deuteronomy 28, verses 1-11, gives a beautiful illustration of God's promises to His children who obey His Word:

"If you fully obey the LORD your God and carefully follow all his commands I give you today, the LORD your God will set you high above all the nations on earth.

All these blessings will come upon you and accompany you if you obey the LORD your God:

You will be blessed in the city and blessed in the country.

The fruit of your womb will be blessed, and the crops of your land and the young of your livestock — the calves of your herds and the lambs of your flocks.

Your basket and your kneading trough will be blessed.

You will be blessed when you come in and blessed when you go out.

The LORD will grant that the enemies who rise up against you will be defeated before you. They will come at you from one direction but flee from you in seven.

The LORD will send a blessing on your barns and on everything you put your hand to. The LORD your God will bless you in the land He is giving you.

The LORD will establish you as His holy people, as He promised you on oath, if you keep the commands of the LORD your God and walk in His ways.

Then all the peoples on earth will see that you are called by the name of the LORD, and they will fear you.

The LORD will grant you abundant prosperity — in the fruit of your womb, the young of your livestock and the crops of your ground — in the land He swore to your forefathers to give you." (NIV)

In today's terminology: When we obey God's commandments, our families, children, homes, jobs, careers, ministries, and bank accounts are prosperous and blessed. God honors his blood covenant with us. He rewards us for our faithfulness and obedience to Christ!!!!!!!!

Christians should discipline themselves to study and meditate on the Word of God so that it transforms their lives. Transformation occurs because God's Word is powerful ... more powerful than our strongholds. **"For the Word of God is quick, and powerful, and sharper than any two-edged sword, piercing even to the dividing asunder of soul and spirit, and of the joints and marrow, and is a discerner of the thoughts and intents of the heart"** (Hebrews 4:12, KJV). Saints of God, if we abide in Christ through obedience to His Word, He will give us the grace (power and ability) to conquer strongholds in our life. It would be wonderful if everything about us instantly changed when we accepted Christ as our Savior. However, that total transformation doesn't occur until we receive our glorified bodies. So while we are on this earth, we must work on renewing our minds and taking care of our physical bodies. This is necessary to experience the fullness of God's promises in His Word. Countless Christians settle only for getting saved and going to heaven when they die. God's desire is for His power and glory to be manifested in our lives on this earth.

I love the book of Ephesians, because in it the Apostle Paul explains the awesome spiritual blessings that come through an intimate relationship with Christ. Ephesians 1:3 states, **"All praise to God, the Father of our Lord Jesus Christ, who has blessed us with every spiritual blessing in the heavenly realms because we are united with Christ"** (NLT). What is also magnificent is that we are each predestined to have an inheritance from God during our stay on this earth and in heaven. **"Furthermore, because we are united with Christ, we have received an inheritance from God, for He chose us in advance, and he makes everything work out according to his plan"**(Ephesians 1:11, NLT). Conquering strongholds helps us each fulfill the call of God on our lives and receive our inheritance.

I didn't know the depth or beauty of what God wanted to do through me until I was free of strongholds. I had taught ladies' Bible study in my church for several years, but God later revealed to me that I was also called to preach His Word. God's power and ability has flowed through me to help deliver other women who had mental strongholds similar to mine. Several years ago a young woman started attending ladies' Bible study at our church. She admitted struggling with depression and stated that she was also prescribed anti-depressant medication. At the time, I was teaching an in-depth study on strongholds. This young woman attended Bible study on a consistent basis and devoured the Word of God. She was very disappointed when we had to cancel Bible study for a season. During her first year of Bible-study attendance, the truth of God's Word, planted in her heart and mind, healed her of depression. Her life was literally transformed before our eyes. She is now facilitating Bible studies and using her spiritual gifts to glorify God.

When we accept Christ as our Savior, we have access to loads of benefits because of our blood covenant with Jesus Christ. Many Christians never enjoy the full benefits of this covenant. Salvation is more than accepting Jesus and going to heaven. In *Grace: The Power of the Gospel*, Andrew Womack also points out that **"salvation is a package deal. It's not only forgiveness from sins, but it includes healing, deliverance and prosperity"** (p. 14). The Bible says that **"I will greatly rejoice in the Lord, my soul shall be joyful in my God; for He hath clothed me with the garments of salvation, He hath covered me with the robe of righteousness, as a bridegroom decketh himself in ornaments, and as a**

bride adorneth herself with her jewels" (Isaiah 61:10, KJV). Garments, to me, represent the coverings and blessings God has provided for his children. Deliverance from strongholds is part of the salvation package.

The Bible also says God has **"delivered us from the power of darkness"** and **"translated us into the Kingdom of his dear Son"** (Colossians 1:13, KJV). Strongholds represent darkness in our lives. Christians were instructed by the Apostle Paul in Romans 12:1-2 to prepare their bodies and minds to honor and please God: **"I beseech you therefore, brethren, by the mercies of God, that ye present your bodies a living sacrifice, holy, acceptable unto God, which is your reasonable service. And be not conformed to this world: but be ye transformed by the renewing of your mind …."** (KJV).

I could not enter in the deeper things of God (peace, joy, health, divine favor, creativity, and revelation knowledge) because of wrong or sinful thought patterns.

I had to get hungry for the things of God and stop trying to appear as though I had it all together. I traded strongholds for the garments of salvation. I hope you decide, while reading this book, that you want **all** your garments of salvation.

CHAPTER 9
Identifying Thoughts and Beliefs That Oppose the Word of God

Now let's take a close look at the thoughts and beliefs we harbor that do not line up with the Word of God. Some of us may feel uncomfortable doing this, but please understand that God loves us unconditionally. *He loves us.* But He hates all sin. Jesus paid the price on Calvary for every sin we will ever commit so that we could have the opportunity to come boldly to God's throne of grace and receive mercy.

The Bible says that the Lord judges us, but we should also judge ourselves. David says in Psalm 26:1-3: **"Judge me, O Lord; for I have walked in mine integrity: I have trusted also in the Lord; therefore I shall not slide. Examine me, O Lord, and prove me; try my reins and my heart. For thy loving kindness is before mine eyes: and I have walked in truth" (KJV)**. David, during this time in his life, wanted God to judge him because he was living righteously. Later on in his life, David committed adultery and eventually murder, but made a decision to judge himself. He repented and asked God to cleanse him from his sin. Here is David's confession in Psalm 51:1-10 (NLT):

> "Have mercy on me, O God, because of your unfailing love. Because of your great compassion, blot out the stains of my sins. Wash me clean from my guilt. Purify me from my sin. For I recognize my rebellion; it haunts me day and night. Against you, and you alone, have I sinned; I have done what is evil in your sight. You will be proved right in what you say,

and your judgment against me is just. For I was born a sinner — yes, from the moment my mother conceived me. But you desire honesty from the womb, teaching me wisdom even there. Purify me from my sins, and I will be clean; wash me, and I will be whiter than snow. Oh, give me back my joy again; you have broken me — now let me rejoice. Don't keep looking at my sins. Remove the stain of my guilt. Create in me a clean heart, O God. Renew a loyal spirit within me."

God showed me in this scripture that His love for us is unfailing and that He is full of compassion. David knew these truths about God. He identified his strongholds and asked God to cleanse him of all unrighteousness. David admitted that he was in rebellion against God's Word, even though he was a man after God's own heart. David's strongholds were rooted in his flesh. He made a decision to kill the sinful desires of his flesh by repenting and drawing close to God. God forgave David and restored his joy in the Lord. But even after all this; David still needed to renew his mind to change the thinking pattern that led him to commit adultery and murder.

David related to God based on an old covenant. Today, we have a better covenant that gives us grace and mercy. Not grace to continue in sin, but grace (power and ability) to live righteously out of love for God. The Greek word for grace is "charis." The objective and subjective meanings of the word grace, or "charis," relate to having favor from someone and also refer to the power and ability to do God's work in ministry (*Vine's Complete Expository Dictionary*). God, in His grace, gave us the Holy Spirit to empower us to live righteous lives. But even with all of God's resources at our disposal, we can still harbor strongholds.

The Bible tells us as Christians to judge ourselves. **"For if we would judge ourselves, we should not be judged. But when we are judged, we are chastened of the Lord, that we should not be condemned with the world"** (1st Corinthians 11:31, KJV). The New Living Translation explains further: *"But if we would examine ourselves, we would not be judged by God in this way. Yet when we are judged by the Lord, we are being disciplined so that we will not be condemned along with the world"* (1st Corinthians 11:31-32.) God does not want us to pay the consequences for sin, as do people who are not saved. However, this will happen if we do not repent. The Bible says that **"the wages of sin is death; but the** gift of God is eternal life through Jesus Christ our Lord" (Romans 6:23, KJV).

Sinful thoughts need to be exposed or admitted to Christ so they can be destroyed by the truth of His Word. When sin is exposed to God, it cannot dwell in His presence. Second Corinthians 10:5 refers to **"casting down imaginations and every high thing that exalteth itself against the knowledge of God, and *bringing into captivity every thought to the obedience of Christ*"** (KJV). It is essential that we **allow** the Holy Spirit to bring ungodly thoughts and beliefs to the **obedience of Christ**. To me, this means making our thoughts agree with God's Word ... or destroying ungodly thoughts with the power of His Word. Ungodly thoughts cannot stay around in the presence of God; however, we must expose them instead of ignore them.

We live in a society that wants us to think there is no absolute truth about what is right or wrong. Some people feel that any action or behavior is O.K. if it makes us feel good, whether it be drugs, alcohol, sex outside of marriage, or getting even with someone. **The world does not want us to refer to a behavior as "sinful" because that means God has a standard by which people should live ... and the world has rejected that standard!** God's standard is for us to be Christ like in our conversations and actions. When we refuse to admit our sinful behaviors, strongholds can develop in our minds. Strongholds have a ripe environment to grow in the minds of people who justify sin.

Thank God for His grace, which allows the blood of Jesus to both wash away our sin and provide forgiveness when we stumble! God sees every sin we commit, but, praise Him; He also sees the blood of Jesus, who paid the price for all sin. Use this time as an opportunity to admit to God any false thinking, fantasies or sinful desires you may have in your life.

Often we fall prey to strongholds because we try to rely on outside forces for our happiness. A woman, for instance, might believe what the Samaritan woman obviously believed — that she must have a man in her life at all times to be happy. This is a belief that opposes the Word of God. God has given us something much better than happiness, and that is His **joy**. The joy that comes from God is not based on our circumstances. It is based on our faith and hope in Jesus Christ.

The Apostle Paul's joy was present during his most difficult circumstances. Consider his advice in Philippians 4:4: **"Always be full of joy in** the Lord. I say it again — rejoice!"** (NLT). The Apostle Paul was in prison when he wrote these words to encourage the Philippian believers. Prisons during this time in history did not have indoor toilets; central heating and air; or privacy. Yet, Paul rejoiced in his spirit because of his relationship with his Lord and Savior, Jesus Christ. Paul did not allow negative thoughts to dominate his thinking and lead him into depression and despair. He was holy (set apart for God in spirit, soul and body).

Several years ago, I went for a 20-minute drive. When I arrived at my destination, I realized I had spent the whole drive thinking about a bad experience I'd gone through more than 15 years earlier. The same feelings I'd harbored then had returned so strongly, it was like the problems had occurred the day before. I realized that I had allowed "old thinking patterns" from previous strongholds to dominate my mind. I allowed thoughts from the past to elevate themselves above the knowledge of God. I knew I should have cast down imaginations and every high thing that had exalted itself against the knowledge of God. Instead of casting the thoughts down, I meditated on them.

This is why it is so important that you monitor your thoughts. Remember … the "mind of the flesh" will try to bring back some of your old struggles and cause you to become angry, worried or upset about something from which you have been delivered. If you are not monitoring your thoughts, the enemy (Satan) may even tempt you to engage in behaviors related to the stronghold.

I like the explanation the *Life Application Study Bible* gives of 2nd Corinthians 10: 4-5: "God must be the commander and chief — even our thoughts must be submitted to His control as we live for Him" (p. 1973). Psalm 139:23-24 bears witness to this explanation: **"Search me, O God, and know my heart: try me, and know my thoughts: And see if there be any wicked way in me, and lead me in the way everlasting"** (KJV). The Holy Spirit within us will reveal sinful or untrue thinking if we spend time with God on a daily basis. During the time I was conquering strongholds, the Holy Spirit would reveal any untrue or vain thoughts in my mind. It was my responsibility to cast down the thought or thought pattern and speak the truth of God's Word. When I began to do this consistently, I was delivered from habitual ungodly thought patterns. Daily renewing of our minds by meditating on the Word of God will help us detect and cast down beliefs and thoughts that disagree with the Word of God.

CHAPTER 10
Come out of Darkness into the Marvelous Light

When my sisters and I were children, we played outside all the time. Our parents would make us come inside when it started getting dark. We were having so much fun playing hide-and-seek or hopscotch, we didn't want to come in the house. We didn't like staying inside when it was daytime or still light outside! When I think back on this time in my life I realize two things: 1) We were children who played during the day, or light, and this was meant to be a time that was good, clean, safe, fun and healthy. 2) We did not play outside at night because of the potential for danger.

The same thing can be applied to our world today in a spiritual sense. We are living in the last days … and these are very challenging times. We must be children of the day, because this is no time to play in the dark. (There are certain places in just about all cities and towns that people avoid visiting after dark.) Some Christians, however, try to be children of both the day and the night. They have one foot in the church and one in the world. This is dangerous because when we choose to sin, we place ourselves under the curse — and Satan can easily attack us. Colossians 1:12-14 says we should be **"always thanking the Father. He has enabled you to share in the inheritance that belongs to his people, who live in the light. For He has rescued us from the kingdom of darkness and transferred us into the Kingdom of His dear Son, who purchased our freedom and forgave our sins"** (NLT). Saints, we have been delivered from darkness and set free, so **why do we still want to play in the dark?** I believe that strongholds in the lives of Christians cause them to play in the dark instead of coming into God's marvelous light. Remember, Jesus paid the price for us to be delivered from darkness. It's a done deal!

Let's examine the strongholds with which numerous people, both Christians and non-Christians, have struggled.

1. Worry

I want to start by telling a true story about myself when I was in my early 20s. I laugh now when I remember the day this event occurred, but at the time it was not funny at all. I had recently given birth to our second and last child. Our children were only 18 months apart. If you know anything about children, you can imagine how tired I was feeling during this time. I was also working full-time. Well, one day I began to worry about how I was feeling. I had convinced myself that I needed to take a short vacation. So I called my mother, told her as much, and said I wanted her to baby-sit her grandchildren.

I must tell you a little about my mother before I give you her answer. My mother was the youngest of four siblings whose parents died before she was a year old. She had a very difficult childhood because she and her siblings grew up very poor. By the grace of God, she managed to complete high school and raise a wonderful family with my father. She was also an exceptionally smart woman who wanted to attend college after high school, but did not have the finances to do so. I was always amazed at her wisdom, because she did not have parents to instill it in her. It had to come from God.

Now, her response to my request.

"I had five children and I never took a vacation until you all were grown," she said. "I think you need to take two aspirin and lay down for a while. You will feel better after you get some rest. I can't keep the children."

I was so disappointed because I had convinced myself, via worry and negative thinking that I could not deal with my children without taking a vacation. Needless to say, I took two aspirin, drank some orange juice and rested for a while. (It was good advice because actually, I wasn't financially able to take a vacation. My husband and I took good care of our children and did not take a vacation until they were much older.)

I was blessed to have a mother with so much godly wisdom. She confronted me with the truth many times, and this helped me to take control over negative thinking and worrying.

I have heard several ministers say that worry is the same as "negative meditation." So we all know how to meditate, because we have all obsessed about something negative! Strongholds can develop when we continually meditate on negative thoughts that oppose the Word of God. When we worry, we are actually allowing a person or situation have **control** over us. God says in His Word that He has equipped us to be controlled by His Spirit within us.

God revealed to me the power of the word **"let"** in the King James Version of the Bible. This small word is crucial in being led by the Holy Spirit. The word **"let"** means to **"give permission or allow"** (*Webster's II New Riverside Desk Dictionary*). A Greek translation of the word "let" is **"apoluo,"** meaning to **"release or set free."** I view this meaning as releasing control of a person or situation to God and freeing the mind to think according to God's Word. Christians must allow the Holy Spirit to empower and help them when struggling with mind battles and temptation to sin. If we begin to meditate on a person or situation, we are being led by our flesh.

When I look back over the things I used to worry about, I realize that 90 percent of the issues were out of my control — things I needed to "release" into God's hands. When I sought God's wisdom and prayed, He reminded me that I didn't have the power to change the person or the situation, but He did.

A favorite scripture that helps me cast down worry and fear is Philippians 4:6: **"Don't worry about anything; instead, pray about everything. Tell God what you need, and thank Him for all He has done"** (NLT). It may seem difficult to not worry about ANYTHING. But that is exactly what God is saying to us. I received a revelation from God that He literally means we are not to worry (be anxious or upset) about any situation. Faith moves the hand of God — not our tears or fears!

The rest of verse 6 tells us how to avoid worrying: by thanking God and making our requests known to Him. Practice thanking God and letting Him know specifically what you desire. He will give you the desires of your heart according to His will. You don't want anything that is not God's will for your life at a given time. You will find that it's much easier to thank God than to worry. And thanking God also pleases Him.

2. **Envy and Jealousy**

Jealousy was another of the strongholds the Holy Spirit and the Word of God helped me to conquer. The root to this stronghold was the fear that

I would never obtain certain things I wanted in life, such as a nice home and financial security. In my earlier years, I was obsessed about purchasing a nice home ... and I admit that I elevated these thoughts above thoughts about God. I became envious and jealous when some close friends of ours bought a nice home. I had problems being happy for them. I felt so ashamed of myself, but something was blocking me from being happy for them. That "something" was a stronghold of jealousy in my mind and heart. The Bible pulls no punches in its assessment of jealousy, as Proverbs 27:4 shows: **"Anger is cruel, and wrath is like a flood, but jealousy is even more dangerous"** (NLT).

It took a minister named Joyce Meyer to help me face this stronghold in my life. One day I heard her admit on national television that she'd previously struggled with jealous thoughts, and that God had delivered her. I was so relieved to hear a minister talk about this issue, because it is rarely discussed in sermons. I had never heard anyone minister on this topic or admit they had problems in this area. I repented and made a decision to renew my mind to agree with God's word. After I repented, God took away all the shame I had felt for so many years because of jealousy in my heart.

The Holy Spirit directed me to study scriptures about jealously. I realized that I had based my happiness on things that were occurring in someone else's life. I thought the other person's life was, in some way, better than mine. Comparing ourselves to other people means that we are leaving out God's standard for our lives. God's Word says our standard should be to **live and love** like Jesus Christ. Ephesians 5:1-2 says to **"imitate God, therefore, in everything you do, because you are his dear children. Live a life filled with love, following the example of Christ. He loved us and offered himself as a sacrifice for us, a pleasing aroma to God"** (NLT). If we have problems with jealousy, we need to renew our minds to the following truth: Jesus gave his life so that **everyone** can have access to an abundant, victorious life in Him. God is not a respecter of persons. It is up to us to choose **life,** which is God's commandment: **"This book of the law shall not depart out of thy mouth; but thou shalt meditate therein day and night, that thou mayest observe to do according to all that is written therein: for then thou shalt make thy way prosperous, and then thou shalt have good success** (Joshua 1:8,

KJV). I like God's **promise** for a successful life if we are obedient. How about you?

One day the Holy Spirit revealed to me that another person's blessings had nothing to do with my blessings — and that I needed to mind my own business! God will never run out of blessings to give His children, but sometimes we act as though there will be nothing left for us. I read the 28th chapter of Deuteronomy and gained wisdom that obedience brings the blessings of God in our lives. This includes outward and inward obedience in our hearts and minds. To have inward obedience, it is essential that we conquer mental strongholds in our lives.

The story of Saul and David in the Bible is a clear example of jealousy and how it will destroy a person's life. Saul became extremely jealous of David's popularity and success, and tried several times to kill David. Let's look at this in 1st Samuel 19:10-12 (KJV): **"And Saul sought to smite David even to the wall with the javelin: but he slipped away out of Saul's presence, and he smote the javelin into the wall: and David fled, and escaped that night. Saul also sent messengers unto David's house, to watch him, and to slay him in the morning: and Michal David's wife told him, saying, If thou save not thy life tonight, tomorrow thou shalt be slain. So Michal let David down though a window: and he went, and fled, and escaped."**

Saul became insanely jealous of David ... to the point that he eventually lost his own life in the process of trying to kill David! Saints of God, harboring jealous thoughts will only destroy us and our relationships. We must deal with jealously when it enters our churches and congregations. We are the Body of Christ, with one Lord and Savior. The Body of Christ cannot be effective when it attacks its own body with jealousy, envy, strife, and hatred. If we did harmful things to our own physical bodies on a regular basis, how well do you think they would function?

3. **Fornication and adultery**

Fornication and adultery are strongholds that are prevalent in the lives of numerous Christians. According to the Web site Freedom Begins Here (**freedombeginshere.com**), seven out of 10 lay leaders in the church, and four out of 10 pastors, have admitted to visiting adult Web sites at least once a week. Freedom Begins Here, which provides resources to help people overcome sexual addictions and pornography, was developed because numerous e-mails were received from pastors and individuals seeking such help, according to Josh Kimball in a Feb. 28, 2009 article, "Christian Artists Address Sex "Crisis" on Tour," at **www.christianpost.com**. We can see from these statistics that even some pastors are struggling with sexual strongholds, and they are seeking help for deliverance.

Roger Rollins, executive director of The Family & Marriage Coalition of Aiken Inc. in Aiken, S.C., and columnist for The *Aiken Standard* (**aikenstandard.com**), reported that more than 45 percent of Christians say pornography is a huge dilemma in their home. And in a nameless survey conducted by **Pastors.com**, 54 percent of pastors admitted looking at pornography during the past year.

It is my opinion that many of these pastors and church leaders feel they have no one to turn to for help in conquering sexual strongholds. And countless pastors avoid teaching against or confronting sexual sins in their congregations to avoid losing ministries or members. This has caused Christians to minimize the harmful effects of sexual sins, and become comfortable with committing fornication and adultery. Brothers and sisters in Christ, our churches need to provide good Bible-based teaching and instruction about the harmful effects of sexual sins in order to help people live holy lives in spirit, soul and body. The **application** of the Word of God is the **best offensive weapon** for tearing down strongholds such as adultery, fornication and pornography.

You may be asking what it means to commit fornication or adultery. Let's define these terms before we go further. **Adultery** is defined in *Nelson's Student Bible Dictionary* as **"willful sexual intercourse with someone other than one's spouse."** (p.7) In Matthew 5:28, according to the dictionary, Jesus expanded the meaning of adultery to include the cultivation of lust: **"'Whoever looks at a woman to lust for her has already committed adultery with her in his heart' "**. The dictionary goes on to define **fornication** as **"sexual relationships outside the bonds of marriage. The technical distinction between fornication and adultery is that adultery involves married persons, while fornication involves at least one person who is unmarried."**

The enemy has built up walls of resistance (fortresses) in the lives of some Christians, and they will actually get angry when confronted about their sexual sins. These Christians are being led by their flesh, and the Bible says our flesh hates God. Romans 8:7 states: **"For the sinful nature is always hostile to God. It never did obey God's laws, and it never** will" (NLT). Simply speaking, Christians who are committing sexual sins are being controlled by their flesh (lower nature). Galatians 5:16-21) speaks specifically about the works of flesh:

> "This I say then, Walk in the Spirit, and ye shall not fulfill the lust of the flesh. For the flesh lusteth against the Spirit, and the Spirit against the flesh: and these are contrary one to the other: so that ye cannot do the things that ye would. But if ye be led of the Spirit, ye are not under the law. Now the works of the flesh are manifest, which are these; Adultery, fornication, uncleanness, lasciviousness, idolatry, witchcraft, hatred, variance, emulations, wrath, strife, seditions, heresies, envyings, murders, drunkenness, revellings, and such like: of the which I tell you before, as I have also told you in time past, that they which do such things shall not inherit the Kingdom of God."(KJV)

The Bible reveals in Romans 8:13 that works of the flesh lead only to death: **"For if you live by its dictates, you will die. But if through the power of the Spirit you put to death the deeds of your sinful nature, you will live"** (NLT).

Fellow Christians, our churches need balanced teaching that helps people address the sins they are committing with their minds and bodies. I say this because we tend to love sermons that focus on the blessings and promises of God, but what about sermons that teach us about the consequences of sin? Christians young and old desperately need teaching about God's commandment to live a sexually pure life, whether you are single or married. The Bible says in Romans 6:13 that we should not yield our members (body parts) as instruments of sin: **"Do not let any part of your body become an instrument of evil to serve sin. Instead, give yourselves completely to God, for you were dead, but now you have new life. So use your whole body as an instrument to do what is right for the glory of God"** (NLT). Our sin nature died with Christ when He was crucified on the cross. This is something many Christians do not know or understand when they accept Christ as their Savior.

The reason some people are not experiencing God's blessings in their lives is because of strongholds such as fornication and adultery. Sexual sins have destroyed countless marriages and families, and this has negatively affected our society as a whole. Just think for a moment about families you know that have been destroyed or devastated because a marriage partner made the choice to have an affair. It is crucial that we stop covering up or ignoring the sexual sins that are prevalent in some of our churches. These types of sins will eventually bring the wrath of God and His judgment. Romans 6:23 says that **"the wages of sin is death, but the gift of God is eternal life through Jesus Christ our Lord"** (KJV). Unfortunately, all too many ministry leaders are reluctant to provide godly counsel to Christians who are engaging in sinful lifestyles.

People need to get hold of the Word of God on a level that brings understanding and deliverance! It is my belief that numerous Christians really do not understand the Bible. I have heard Christians say, "I tried to read the Bible, but I could not understand the King James Version." That's no excuse, because the Word comes in a number of easy-to-read versions nowadays. I admit that in my earlier years it was difficult for me to understand the King James Version of the Bible. One day I decided to purchase the *Life Application Study Bible* to help increase my understanding. This was the best decision I had made in quite some time. The *Life Application Study Bible* greatly increased my understanding of God's Word and how to apply it in my life. I began to desire more of God's Word. Studying its truths on a level I could understand helped me conquer strongholds in my life. (It also helped greatly that I **wanted to be free** of strongholds that blocked my spiritual growth.)

The Ten Commandments reveal our sin nature before we accept Christ as Savior. They point out that we have all sinned and fallen short of the glory of God no matter how **good we think we are**. God's Word is the **only truth** that will **destroy** strongholds. Frequently, Christians avoid talking about strongholds because they fear condemnation. Paul stated in Romans 8:1 that **"there is therefore now no condemnation to them which are in Christ Jesus, who walk not after the flesh, but after the Spirit"** (KJV). Jesus said that He came to save, not to condemn. (John 3:17). Since Jesus came to save us and not condemn us, we need to address strongholds in our lives so we can be in close relationship with our Savior and Lord.

If committing sexual sins is one of your strongholds, remember the Samaritan woman and how Jesus changed her life! She gained a Savior and gladly gave up the sexual sins in her life. She allowed Jesus (the Word) to heal the root of her stronghold, which was low self-esteem. I strongly suggest that you prayerfully determine the root to your stronghold and allow the Holy Spirit to minister to you in this area. Deliverance has already been provided for you through Christ Jesus. You must decide to accept your deliverance and walk in liberty and freedom from sexual sin. Galatians 5:1 instructs us to **"stand fast therefore in the liberty wherewith Christ hath made us free, and be not entangled again with the yoke of bondage"** (KJV).

4. Addiction

Addiction is one of the major strongholds in the lives of Christians and non-Christians alike. The definition of "addiction," for the purpose of this book, is "to surrender one's self habitually or compulsively" to a substance (*Webster's II New Riverside Desk Dictionary*). I chose this definition because it plainly shows the habitual nature of a stronghold in a person's life, and how a person can surrender to the stronghold. Addiction also refers to dependence on a substance or substances. M.A. Schuckit, in his book *Drug and Alcohol Abuse: A Clinical Guide to Diagnosis and Treatment*, defines dependence as a "psychological and/or physical need for the drug" (p. 9).

This fast-paced society, with its microwave and drive-through meals, has us thinking we can fix major problems in our lives in just a few minutes. This is one reason numerous individuals turn to substances for relief from pain or stress. People who smoke, for instance, report that cigarettes calm them and help them deal with stress. Many of us enjoy our caffeinated coffee in the morning to help us feel more alert and ready to start the day. We like those quick fixes, so to speak. But for how long are we fixed?

Countless individuals spend years of their lives addicted to cigarettes, alcohol, cocaine, prescription drugs, food and/or pornography. This dependency on substances becomes a way of life to these individuals. Their lifestyles do not agree with God's Word and are therefore not pleasing to Him. The truth is, they have strongholds that need to be conquered. And before a conquest can take place, the "roots" of the strongholds must be addressed.

If you are reading this book and you are addicted to a substance, know that deliverance is available to you. God paid the price for all sin, sickness and disease on Calvary. If you are already a Christian, you have already been delivered from darkness! Now is the time to repent and begin to renew your mind so that you can walk in the light of God's word.

Granted, addictions can be some of the most difficult strongholds to conquer. I have known of people who were instantly delivered from addictions and others who required more time to completely eliminate the addictions from their lives. The born- again spirit (our new nature) desires to please God. However, if the spirit is not built up and fed the Word of God regularly, the flesh can dominate the "new nature" to get what it wants. When our minds are not renewed, we make choices to follow our fleshly desires instead of our new nature.

When we are dealing with problems, God desires that we seek wisdom from Him instead of turning to a drug to cope. When Christians refuse to deal with an addiction, they have elevated the desire for a substance above the desire for God.

Whether His deliverance is instant or whether He chooses to help through professionals with special training, God wants to be the One to whom we turn for peace, joy, help, comfort and healing from strongholds of addiction.

5. Unforgiveness

Unforgiveness is epidemic in today's society. Many Christians have harbored unforgiveness toward others for decades and are not even aware of it! This is clearly a way of thinking that is against the Word of God. Unforgiveness is like a mental fortress that blocks God's Word from penetrating the heart to bring healing. The person harboring unforgiveness has difficulty releasing, or letting go, of his hurt or pain.

In the teaching titled "Three O'clock in the Morning," Perry Stone explained that the word "fortress" refers to a prison in the Greek translation. He pointed out that a fortress and a prison both have walls. The walls of a fortress are designed to prevent anyone from entering the fortress, and the walls of a prison are designed to prevent anyone from leaving the prison. This explanation made sense to me when I applied it to strongholds. When we have strongholds in our minds, there are fortress walls that try to block the Word of God from entering our hearts and minds, while the prison walls try to prevent the strongholds from leaving our minds and our emotions.

I thank our all-powerful God that His Word will penetrate any prison wall or fortress. Here is a scripture that ministered to me in the area of unforgiveness:

"Then came Peter to him, and said, Lord, how oft shall my brother sin against me, and I forgive him? till seven times? Jesus saith unto him, I say not unto thee, Until seven times: but, Until seventy times seven" (Matthew 18:21-22, KJV). Jesus was clearly instructing Peter, and us, to have hearts and minds set on forgiving others, regardless of the number of times we have to forgive them! I am not saying we will never have problems forgiving. Sometimes we will struggle with it. Just think about the fact that Jesus forgave us for all our sins ... and we have certainly hurt others in some way during our lifetime.

The Lord's Prayer actually states, **"And forgive us our debts, AS we forgive our debtors"** (Matthew 6:12, KJV). Debts, in this sense, are defined as sins. The New Living Translation states this verse as **"And forgive us our sins *as* we have forgiven those who sin against us."** The word "as" is italicized to emphasize its meaning, which is "to the same degree or extent, equally" (TheFreeDictionary.com). We receive God's forgiveness for our sins *to the same degree* that we forgive others. This scripture made me realize how easy it is for each of us to have our own standard of righteousness, when our standard should be God's commandment.

In her book *Jesus: The One and Only*, Beth Moore shared a perspective about forgiveness among Christians that I had not considered. She states that Christians should be mature enough to speak the truth in love (Ephesians 4:15) to each other, even if that means rebuking or receiving a rebuke from a fellow Christian. This perspective, to me, shows the depth of love we should have for one another.

Another scripture that focuses on mature Christians as it relates to forgiveness is Matthew 5:44-45. It states, **"But I say unto you, Love your enemies, bless them that curse you, do good to them that hate you, and pray for them which despitefully use you, and persecute you; that ye may be the children of your Father which is in heaven: for He maketh His sun to rise on the evil and on the good, and sendeth rain on the just and on the unjust"** (KJV). Just imagine, for a moment, the sun rising only on good people. Can you imagine what a sunny day would look like? There would be areas of sunlight and darkness within a few feet, or inches, of each other. What a strange-looking sunny day that would be!

Minister Teresia Dupins

God is so merciful and loving that He allows everyone (sinners and saints) to receive His rain and sunshine. As Christians, we radiate the sunlight of God when we love and forgive others.

IV: How to Conquer Strongholds

CHAPTER 11
Programming Your New Nature and Renewing Your Mind

I was a teenager in the 1970s. Our family was at church pretty much every time the doors were open. We were blessed to attend a church that helped us understand the importance of accepting Jesus Christ as our Savior. We also learned to have a deep reverence for God (both awe of Him and fear of committing certain sins). But in our local churches at the time, there was very little, if any, teaching available about the soul and spirit. We thought the spirit and the soul were one and the same. We did not understand the "new nature" we each received after accepting Christ. And we certainly did not know that the "old sin nature" was dead, regardless of sins we committed. Several Christians in our church continued committing the same sins after accepting Christ. They tried to make up for their sins by coming to the front of the altar and "verbally rededicating" their lives. But this action did not help conquer the strongholds.

In a church service we may become emotional during a song or sermon, but there was rarely any true deliverance from strongholds such as jealousy, unforgiveness, hatred, addiction, fornication, adultery and worry.

I mentioned earlier that the first time I heard teaching about jealously in the body of Christ was when I heard Joyce Meyer minister on television in the late 1990s. I was 38 years old when I heard this information. I sincerely wish I had received it earlier in my life! This is one of the reasons I wrote this book ... so that Christians young and old can receive more of this type teaching and be delivered from strongholds in their lives.

As we begin this chapter, let's think about the computers in our homes and/or offices. Remember using a computer for the first time? There were so many programs that we were unfamiliar with, or did not know existed. A whole new way of communicating was available to us. We had more information than we could access in a lifetime. Therefore, our computers needed to be programmed with the information we specifically wanted for our work or personal use.

In the world of computers, the word "program" means to schedule, design, or arrange information. Let's look at how we can conquer strongholds by programming our "new nature" (born-again spirit) with the correct information, which is God's Word. The Bible says that **"thy word is a lamp unto my feet and a light unto my path"** (Psalm 119:105, KJV). If God's Word is a lamp that gives us light to guide our steps, we must certainly program our new nature with that information. Philippians 2:5 states, **"Let this mind be in you, which was also in Christ Jesus"** (KJV). Programming our new nature with the Word of God is letting (allowing and placing) God's Word into our hearts and minds (through reading and studying) so we can use that information in our everyday lives.

When our "new nature" is programmed correctly, we can respond to temptations, challenges and difficult situations in a godly manner. We are also equipping ourselves to tear down the strongholds (thoughts, behaviors and lifestyles) that are against God's Word. Paul is a wonderful example of a Christian who programmed his new nature to respond to difficult situations and adversity. In Philippians 1:12-14, Paul states from prison, **"And I want you to know, my dear brothers and sisters, that everything that has happened to me here has helped to spread the Good News. For everyone here, including the whole palace guard, knows that I am in chains because of Christ. And because of my imprisonment, most of the believers here have gained confidence and boldly speak God's message without fear"** (NLT).

I believe Paul had to diligently meditate (think seriously, dwell, reflect) upon the Word of God to be able to speak so boldly while he was in prison. Just think about the horrible conditions of prisons during this time in history. There were no modern conveniences such as central air and heat, indoor toilets or aerosol air fresheners. Despite these horrible living conditions Paul stated in Philippians 3:10 **"I want to KNOW Christ and experience the mighty power that raised Him from the dead"** (NLT).

What a long way Paul had come! Before he was saved, Paul, formerly known as Saul, had a way of thinking that did not agree with God's Word. He had elevated the law above having a relationship with Jesus Christ. Therefore, he had a mental stronghold that prevented God's power from flowing in his life. After his conversion on the road to Damascus (Acts 9), Paul programmed his new nature to respond like Christ through study, prayer and application of the Word of God. During his lifetime he was beaten, thrown into prison, shipwrecked and left for dead. But Paul endured, because he did not wait for a crisis in his life to call on God or read or study His Word. He was always ready to give a godly response to believers and unbelievers. He had conquered the strongholds in his life. His new nature was programmed with the powerful Word of God to conquer every adversity he faced. I don't know about you, but I want to program my new nature to respond the same way!

Don't allow strongholds in your life to block spiritual growth or fellowship with God. Begin to read and study the Word of God daily, even if it is only for five minutes at a time in your bathroom. It works for me. I have a stack of Christian magazines and books in a magazine rack right beside the toilet. All I have to do is reach down, pick up something and start reading. This is one of my ways of programming my "new nature." (My first cousin says people can "get saved" in my bathroom.)

The word of God tells us to meditate on the word day and night and we will be successful. Start today reaching for the Word of God and program your new nature!

CHAPTER 12
Deleting Old Sinful Data

Now that you have knowledge of programming your new nature by renewing your mind, it is time to focus on deleting old data ... wrong thinking patterns, imaginations, negative emotions, and behaviors related to strongholds in your life. Our "old sin nature" died with Christ and we have a brand-new nature, which is our born-again spirit. Deleting old data removes areas in the soul (mind, will and emotions) that our flesh us**es** to keep us in bondage to strongholds.

    I believe some Christians are still feeding their strongholds in secret. Many a Christian will hide a stronghold in his life until a situation happens that exposes his habitual sinful behavior to the public. I remember a sermon my husband preached, titled "The Secret Storms." He said the secret storms are the strongholds and issues in our lives that we keep hidden from others, i.e., sexual affairs or addictions to drugs or food. Many Christians know that they have been delivered from their sin nature, but don't realize they must crucify the sin that lies in their flesh (soul and body). I believe that crucifying our flesh also means using our spiritual weapons to deny the flesh's right to control us.

    The Bible says that we have spiritual weapons that help us delete old data (including things we keep hidden) and conquer strongholds: **"For the weapons of our warfare are not carnal, but mighty through God to the pulling down of strongholds"** (2nd Corinthians 10:4, KJV). The world uses natural weapons, both tangible (guns, knives) and intangible (cursing, fighting, backbiting, lying, hating). The spiritual weapons God has given us are more powerful, because greater is He that is within us than he that is within the world (1st John 4:4). These spiritual weapons include **prayer, faith, love, peace, a joyful spirit, minding the things of the spirit,** and of course, **His spoken Word** (Philippians 4; Galatians 5:22-25). Spiritual weapons may seem useless to those of us who are dealing with difficult situations or strongholds in our lives. But this is exactly what the enemy wants us to think.

I remember two specific times in my life when strife and confusion arose on my job and certain individuals hurt me. I was tempted to say and do things out of my flesh, but God reminded me to use my spiritual weapons … and told me to be a blessing, through giving, to the very individuals by whom I'd been hurt. At first my flesh rebelled. But as soon as I gave, I felt a freedom that only comes from God. Now had I chosen to use worldly weapons, the situations would have worsened. Instead, I chose to use spiritual weapons, demonstrating love to those who had hurt me. And God turned the entire situation around for good, bringing healing to me and to the other individuals.

The enemy wants to keep people from obeying God's commandments because he knows that obedience brings God's power, protection and blessings. We need to use our spiritual weapons because they give us the ability to pull down everything in our lives that does not agree with the Word of God.

Our spiritual weapons also include the armor God says we should put on every day to guard against attacks from the devil. This armor is located in the book of Ephesians 6, verses 13-17: **"Therefore, put on every piece of God's armor so you will be able to resist the enemy in the time of evil. Then after the battle you will still be standing firm. Stand your ground, putting on the belt of truth and the body armor of God's righteousness. For shoes, put on the peace that comes from the Good News so that you will be fully prepared. In addition to all of these, hold up the shield of faith to stop the fiery arrows of the devil. Put on salvation as your helmet, and take the sword of the spirit, which is the Word of God"** (NLT). Isn't it wonderful to know that God has already equipped us with spiritual weapons and armor to tear down strongholds and prevent them from returning? Every day we need to put on our spiritual clothing, which includes the belt of truth, the breastplate of righteousness, shoes of peace, the shield of faith and the helmet of salvation. God designed our armor to protect every part of the body and mind! Saints of God, we just need to get up every day and put on the armor by praying, confessing the Word of God and making the choice to live righteously.

Deleting old data most certainly involves renewing our minds with the Word of God. I know that I have mentioned renewing the mind numerous times throughout this book, but I can't emphasize it enough … renewing the mind is **essential** to conquering strongholds. We must replace old data with new data that feeds our born-again spirit (Romans 12:1-2). The renewing of our minds brings about transformation and equips us to do the will of God and live by the Spirit.

Paul was a born-again Christian when he talked about the struggle he had with his flesh. He knew that the desire to do what was right was within his born-again spirit, but he had to crucify his flesh. He found out that the only way to do this was through Christ: **"O wretched man that I am! Who shall deliver me from the body of this death? I thank God through Jesus Christ our Lord. So then with the mind I myself serve the law of God; but with the flesh the law of sin"** (Romans 7:24-25, KJV). Let's examine the seventh chapter of Romans to see how Paul deleted old data that was in his flesh:

Paul exposed the sin that was in his flesh. He did not keep it a secret like some of us do just because we are Christians (verses 18-19).

Paul confessed that he delighted in the law of God after his born-again spirit (verse 22).

He acknowledged another law in the members of his body (the flesh), warring against the law of the mind. Our mind makes the decision of whether or not to sin. Therefore, in his mind, Paul made the decision not to sin (verse 23).

Paul crucified the sin nature of his flesh through Jesus Christ. He **chose** *to serve God rather than his flesh. He made a conscious decision to obey God's Word in every circumstance (verse 25).*

Every time we make the choice to obey God's Word rather than please our flesh, we are chipping away at old habits and negative thinking patterns. The Holy Spirit then empowers us to do the will of God during situations in which we are tempted to sin. As we begin to desire more and more of God's Word, old data is deleted and we have more space on our computer hard drives for new data (the Word of God).

CHAPTER 13
Entering New Data: The Word of God

"**Let this mind be in you, which was also in Christ Jesus**" (Philippians 2:5). Just look at the progress you have made so far on this journey to become who God has created you to be! You now have an understanding about strongholds, knowledge about programming your new nature, and knowledge about deleting old data that lead to sin. Now it is time enter new data in your new nature to conquer strongholds.

Numerous Christians are starving spiritually. On the outside they may look healthy, but on the inside their spirits are malnourished and in need of the Word of God. John 1:1 says that **"in the beginning was the Word, and the Word was with God, and the Word was God"** (KJV). When we enter the Word of God into our spirits and minds, we are entering the power of God to conquer strongholds. New data equips the soul to make godly decisions that agree with the born-again spirit.

Let's view programming our new nature similar to the way we input data in our computers via their hard drives. Spiritually speaking, let's call the hard drive the "spirit and mind." The first step is to enter the correct information, data or material on the hard drive. This information is the truth of God's Word about every situation we are dealing with in our lives. We want this information to always be available at our fingertips because it helps us obey God's Word with ease. God helps us handle strongholds and other difficulties in life with a spirit of ease if we allow Him. Jesus said in Matthew 11:28-30: **"Come unto me, all ye that labour and are heavy laden, and I will give you rest. Take my yoke upon you and learn of me; for I am meek and lowly in heart: and ye shall find rest unto your**

souls. For my yoke is easy and my burden is light"(KJV). From this scripture, I see three things Jesus is instructing us to do: 1) Come to Him, 2) Take His yoke (his spiritual weapons and armor), and 3) Learn of Him (renew our minds by entering new data).

To apply this concept in a spiritual sense, the information we each put on our hard drive (spirit and mind) depends on the type of stronghold we desire to conquer and prevent from returning. For instance, a stronghold of low self-esteem can be defeated by the input (confession and meditation on) the following affirmations and scriptures:

God's love for me is everlasting	Jeremiah 31:3
I am fearfully and wonderfully made	Psalm 139:14
I have been cleansed of all my sins	Ephesians 1:7
I am without fault before God	Ephesians 1:4
God loves me	John 3:16
God created me to triumph in Hi	2nd Corinthians 2:14
I can do all things through Christ which strengthens me	Philippians 4:13
God's spirit lives within me	1st Corinthians 6:19

What if a person has a stronghold related to his sexuality and desires deliverance from this stronghold? To begin with, he must believe in his heart that this lifestyle opposes the Word of God. This is the initial step in tearing down the fortress/wall in his mind. The next step is entering new data, which is God's Word about that sin or stronghold. Lastly, the person must desire to have godly sorrow about the sin and repent (completely turn away) from the sin.

Homosexuality, for instance is a lifestyle that opposes the Word of God. Romans 1:26-27 states, **"That is why God abandoned them to their shameful desires. Even the women turned against the natural way to have sex and instead indulged in sex with each other. And the men, instead of having normal sexual relations with women, burned with lust for each other. Men did shameful things with other men, and as a result of this sin, they suffered within themselves the penalty they deserved"** (NLT).

The truth of God's Word is in Genesis 1:27-28a: **"So God created man in His own image, in the image of God created He him;** male and female **created He them. And God blessed** them, **and God said unto**

them, Be fruitful and multiply ...." (KJV). God created the male and female, and He blessed them and commanded them to be fruitful and multiply. God's blessing is on marriage between a male and female, not two males or two females. It takes a male sperm and a female egg joined together to create a human life.

Now Satan cannot create anything. Remember, he had the first stronghold and wanted to be like God. All Satan can do is abuse and distort what God has already created. And there are people today who have figured out ways to make it look as though they can create life. Just within the past few years there was a man on a television show who was pregnant. How could this be? Well, the man was actually born a woman. She decided to become a man and had several "sex-change" procedures done to *look* like a man, but kept her uterus to reproduce. This is one example of how Satan distorts God's creation for his own purposes. Satan influences people to use the media to glorify sin and desensitize people to sin so that they will begin accepting alternative lifestyles.

The Bible states that **"in the last days perilous times shall come. For men shall be lovers of their own selves, covetous, boasters, proud, blasphemers, disobedient to parents, unthankful, unholy, without natural affection, trucebreakers, false accusers, incontinent, fierce, despisers of those that are good, traitors, heady, highminded, lovers of pleasures rather than lovers of God"** (2nd Timothy 3:1b-4, KJV). Doesn't this scripture give a clear illustration of the sin in our world today? Look at the countless people who are more concerned about pleasing themselves than God.

Dr. Harry Schaumburg, in his book *False Intimacy: Understanding the Struggle of Sexual Addiction*, has this to say about homosexuality and other deviant sexual behaviors: "... The origin of sexual deviant behavior, including homosexuality and sexual addiction, is in the deceitful human heart, not in one's painful circumstances or abusive childhood. When we understand the plague that is in the human heart, all other views of the origin of immoral sexual behavior are set aside. The problem is not sexual addiction or sexual confusion; it is sin" (p.53). *Many* people who have strongholds are unwilling to admit that sin is the problem. When I struggled with strongholds in my own life, I did not want to admit that sin was the problem. However, when I began to study and meditate on scriptures in the Bible, God revealed to me the sinful thought patterns in my mind. To break down these thought patterns, I entered new data … the truth of who I am in Christ Jesus. I was strengthening my brand-new nature that was free from sin. God said that I was more than a conqueror through Christ, who'd strengthened me. His Word revealed that He had plans to make me a success (Joshua 1:7-9). I habitually meditated on the Word of God to keep this new data on my hard drive.

Let's return to our discussion about the person who has a stronghold of homosexuality or sexual addiction, and enter some new data:

1. "Therefore if any man be in Christ, he is a new creature: old things are passed away; behold all things are become new" (2nd Corinthians 5:17, KJV).
2. I am alive in Christ and no longer controlled by a sin nature (Romans 6:11).
3. I use my body to glorify God. I am alive from the dead (Romans 6:13).
4. I think like Christ. Therefore I do what pleases Him (1st Corinthians 2:16).
5. God loves me (John 3:16).
6. God's temple dwells in my spirit and His temple is holy (1st Corinthians 3:17).
7. I meditate on true, pure, honest, lovely thoughts (Philippians 4:8).
8. I have put on the new man who is like my Creator, the righteous and holy God (Ephesians 4:24).
9. I walk in the Spirit and I do not fulfill the lust of my flesh (Galatians 5:16).
10. I fear (reverence) the Lord and I depart from evil (Proverbs 3:7).

We can find plenty of scriptures in the Bible to help us change our thinking patterns and conquer any stronghold!

Dr. Caroline Leaf, in her book *Who Switches off My Brain: Controlling Toxic Thoughts and Emotions*, says something very powerful about thoughts: "If they are powerful enough to make us sick, they are powerful enough to make us healthy as well" *(p.108)*. God tells us in His Word to control our thoughts by renewing our minds. We have the ability to conquer strongholds by changing what we meditate on and think about. Every stronghold has thought patterns associated with it; these thought patterns can lead to sickness and sin.

Dr. Leaf states we have the ability to "build a strong memory" by refusing to accept toxic or negative thoughts. She elaborates on how this helps detoxify our brains so we can build good, strong memories that promote health (p. 115).

I am not saying that conquering strongholds such as homosexuality and pornography will be as simple as meditating on a few scriptures each day. I believe that each person should pray and seek God's guidance on how to obtain godly counsel in conquering these strongholds. This counsel may come from mature believers in Christ who have overcome the specific stronghold the person desires to conquer, and/or from Christian books that focus on the stronghold.

Entering new data (God's Word) is like cleansing our brains of thoughts that strengthen the strongholds in our lives. Meditating on the Word of God, confessing it out loud, and refusing to yield to temptations to sin will tear down walls that support the fortresses in our minds. When the walls fall down, new data (God's Word) enter our spirits and minds. And sinful thought patterns and beliefs (old data) can exit!

V Making God Your Only Stronghold

CHAPTER 14
Delighting Yourself in the Lord

"Delight thyself also in the Lord: and He shall give thee the desires of thine heart" (Psalm 37:4, KJV).

It is my belief that many strongholds develop through an attempt to meet a need or desire. It may be a tangible need. It may be a need for love or a need to relieve emotional pain. It may be a desire to achieve something worthwhile. In actuality, we are in a vicious cycle trying to please our flesh … which can never be satisfied. The Bible says that if we delight ourselves in the Lord, He will give us our hearts' desires. Of course this means He will give us these desires according to His will and purpose for our lives. Desire means "to hope or wish for ardently, crave, and a strong wish or longing" (*Webster's II Desk Dictionary*). In essence, the Bible is saying that we each are to have a strong longing for the Lord and **crave to spend time fellowshipping with Him**. Our greatest hope should be in our Lord and Savior, Jesus Christ. When we delight in the Lord in this manner, we will most certainly conquer strongholds. Just imagine all Christians in the world craving and longing to spend time with the Lord throughout the day! What a beautiful display of the Kingdom of God this would be!

A major key to my victory over strongholds was learning to delight myself in the Lord. I got to the point where I wanted to please God more than I wanted anything else in life. When I was tempted to think or act against God's Word, I said to myself, *"I Love God More."* I truly wanted to please

God with my spirit, soul and body. When I made the decision to please God, the Holy Spirit empowered me to obey God instead of my flesh.

The Bible says that your obedience to God shows your love for Him: **"If ye love me, keep my commandments"** (John 14:15, KJV). It is so much easier to obey God when you have learned to delight in Him. Remember when you were in love the first time and how you wanted to please that person? Well, falling in love with Jesus and delighting in your relationship with Him will cause you to want to please Him. Your desire for things in the world (drugs, pornography, alcohol, material things) will begin to decrease as you get closer to God, because He will get closer to you. **"Draw nigh to God, and He will draw nigh to you. Cleanse your hands, ye sinners; and purify your hearts, ye double minded"** (James 4:8, KJV). God desires that Christians fellowship with Him on a continual basis, just as in the Garden of Eden before Adam and Eve sinned. However, many Christians who have strongholds are double minded. They are trying to fit in the world *and* in the Kingdom of God. Having carnal (worldly) minds blocks their desire to "draw nigh to God" and fellowship with Him.

As I began to write this book, God revealed to me that He is the **only** stronghold we, as Christians, should have in our lives. He wants to be the one we habitually run to for fellowship and assistance in facing difficult situations.

I searched the Bible for scriptures to support what God had revealed to me and found the following:
1. **"The Lord is good, a stronghold in the day of trouble; and He knoweth them that trust in him"** (Nahum 1:7, KJV).
2. **"Be thou my strong habitation, whereunto I may continually resort: thou hast given commandment to save me; for thou art my rock and my fortress."** (Psalm 71:3, KJV).

Some points to meditate on:
1. God is the only fortress or fortified place we should have in our minds. He is our habitation and dwelling place. We are to dwell in the secret place of the Most High God (Psalm 91:1).
2. When faced with challenges, we should seek Him first because His Word says He has provided protection for the righteous. Psalm 34:17 states that **"the righteous cry, and the Lord heareth, and delivereth them out of all their troubles"** (KJV).

3. **"I will say of the Lord, He is my refuge and my fortress: my God; in Him will I trust"** (Psalm 91:2, KJV). Again, we see that God is to be the fortress in our minds and hearts. If we have any stronghold other than God, it must be torn down.
4. **"I have set the Lord always before me: because He is at my right hand, I shall not be moved"** (Psalm 16:8, KJV). When the Lord is our stronghold, we turn to Him to meet our needs and desires.
5. **"The name of the Lord is a strong tower: the righteous runneth into it, and is safe"** (Proverbs 18:10, KJV).
6. **"For the weapons of our warfare are not carnal, but mighty through God to the pulling down of strongholds"** (2nd Corinthians 10:4, KJV).

When God is the only stronghold in our lives, we will habitually seek God and obey His commandments. Habitual fellowship with God is the best way to become spiritually mature. The enemy (Satan) knows that mature Christians are a threat to his kingdom, so he tries continually to distract us from reading, studying, praying or confessing the Word of God. I am not saying that it is always the devil's fault that we do not study the Word or pray. In many cases, we simply have the wrong priorities in life and have not disciplined ourselves to study. This just makes it easier for the enemy to distract us from spending time with God.

Another thing to remember is that we must avoid seeking pleasure from sinful habits or lifestyles. With God as our only stronghold, we derive our deepest pleasure from spending time with Him.

Now that you have gained awareness about entering new data in your spirit and mind, here is a step-by-step process for making God your only stronghold:

Admit that you have strongholds in your life.

Focus on developing your relationship with the Lord. A close relationship with the Lord will cause you to love Him with your whole heart, soul and mind. (Matthew 22:37).

Join a church that helps you understand the Word of God and apply it in your life.

Confess that God is your only stronghold, using these scriptures: Psalm 91:2, Psalm 71:3 and others mentioned in the above section.

Forgive those who have hurt you. Love, pray for and bless your enemies. (Matthew 5:44).

> *Desire to live a holy life, pleasing to God in spirit, soul and body. (1st Thessalonians 5:23; 1st Peter 2:5).*
> *Renew your mind with the Word of God. Find scriptures related to the areas you struggle in, and confess them out loud. Write out your own scriptural affirmations for becoming who God created you to be. (Romans 12:1-2).*
> *Desire to be rooted and grounded in the love of Christ Jesus. He will help you defeat the roots to the strongholds. (Ephesians 3:17-19)*
> *Set your mind on Christ so that any thought that disagrees with the Word of God will be exposed and cast down. (2nd Corinthians 10: 3-5).*
> *Abide (dwell, stay) in Christ. (John 15:7, Psalm 91:1-2).*
> *Guard your mind from evil. (1st Thessalonians 5:22, Romans 12:9).*
> *Ask God to help you use your spiritual gifts to glorify Him and bless others.*
> *Confess the Word out loud and say what God says about you.*

The Bible shares other ways to delight in the Lord. One way is boasting in the Lord: **"My soul shall make her boast in the Lord: the humble shall hear thereof, and be glad. O magnify the Lord with me, and let us exalt his name together"** (Psalm 34: 2-3, KJV). If we learned to boast in the Lord and magnify Him throughout the day on a consistent basis, our delight would be in Him and not sinful habits or lifestyles. What if Adam and Eve had boasted in the Lord when Satan first tempted them to question God's instructions to them? I believe they would have obeyed God, taken authority over Satan and kicked him out of the garden.

The Apostle Paul faced much difficulty in his life. One of the ways he dealt with persecution was to rejoice in the Lord. **"Always be full of joy in the Lord. I say it again — rejoice!"** (Philippians 4:4, NLT). Paul always chose to be full of the joy of the Lord, regardless of his circumstances. If Paul had given up the first time he was persecuted for the cause of Christ, we would not have two-thirds of the New Testament that God inspired him to write! Paul was able to persevere because God was his ONLY stronghold … his joy and his peace. You can choose to make God your only stronghold by making a decision to desire God more than you desire anything else in this world. Believe His Word, confessing it over your life. And — last but not least — continually rejoice and boast in the Lord.

CHAPTER 15
Living Holy and Righteously

"For He hath made Him to be sin for us, who knew no sin; that we might be made the righteousness of God in [Christ Jesus]" (2nd Corinthians 5:21, KJV).

I spent several years of my life lacking the full understanding that God, through Jesus Christ, had made me holy and righteous. In addition, I needed an understanding of what it meant to **live** holy and righteously. I loved God and was using some of my gifts to help others, but I was not free to be who God created me to be. What I am saying is that it was easy for me to "talk the talk," but I had to also learn how to "walk the walk." God desires that Christians display *victorious* lifestyles, not the lifestyles of people without a relationship with God. Conquering strongholds in my life set me on the path for abundant living in the Kingdom of God. I was set free from ungodly thought patterns that dominated my thought life and limited my ability to be led by the Spirit of God. Dear friend, this is God's desire for you too.

Let's revisit some of the scenarios that I shared in the Introduction of the book. Pastor Glover succumbed to adultery after ten years of successful ministry. Polly succumbed to abusing alcohol after becoming a successful investment banker. You may wonder how this could happen after years of success. One of the main reasons is that these individuals denied or did not know how about the strongholds in their lives. The root or roots to their strongholds also needed to be exposed and destroyed. The Bible tells us we must judge ourselves or we will be judged by God: **"For if we would judge ourselves, we should not be judged. But when** we are judged, we are chastened of the Lord, that we should not be condemned with the world"** (1st Corinthians 11:31-32, KJV).

If we do not deal with our wrong thinking or sinful habits, they will eventually resurface during times of stress, adversity, boredom or temptation. These individuals were able to be effective in ministry for a while, but strongholds blocked their ability to live holy and righteously according to God's word when faced with temptation or challenges.

You may be wondering, "So what does it mean to live holy and righteously?" The word "holy" is described as sanctification and "set-apartness" for service to God (*Vine's Complete Expository Dictionary*, p. 307). I understand this to mean that my soul (mind, will, emotions), body and heart are to be set apart to glorify God (1st Thessalonians 5:23). First Peter 1:15-16 elaborates even further: **"But now you must be holy in everything you do, just as God who chose you is holy. For the Scriptures say, you must be holy because I am holy"** (NLT).

We can all attest to the fact that the lives of many Christians are definitely not set apart for God's service. Many of us in the body of Christ are a long way from being holy in "everything we do." But I believe that God would not ask us to do something that is impossible. It is entirely possible to live holy and righteously through Christ, which Paul discovered at the end of the seventh chapter of Romans as well as in Chapter 8. First Thessalonians 4:7-8 also tells us that **"God has called us to live holy lives, not impure lives. Therefore, anyone who refuses to live by these rules is not disobeying human teaching but is rejecting God, who gives his Holy Spirit to you"** (NLT). God gave us his Holy Spirit to equip us to "live holy." Saints of God, we have the power within us to be holy as God is holy. This may sound boring or even scary to some people, but living holy is actually the most exhilarating thing a Christian can experience on a daily basis. This is because we are allowing Christ to live through us and through our unique personalities. There is freedom and liberty in living holy. Hallelujah!!!!!

Since God predestined for us to be made the righteousness of Him in Christ Jesus, we certainly need to know what righteousness means. *Nelson's Student Bible Dictionary* defines righteousness as "holy and upright living in accordance with God's standard" (p. 223). I don't know about you, but for many years I was somewhat self-righteous. I took pride in the fact that I didn't drink, steal, sleep around, curse people or go to nightclubs.

This made me feel that I wasn't as bad as some Christians, or those who were not saved. However, I was deceived in my thinking because it was only the grace of God that made me righteous. At the time I wasn't willing to admit sins of jealousy, envy, gluttony and vanity. I had also minimized my ungodly thought patterns, which could not be seen by others.

Living righteously also means that our thought lives are pleasing to God. This is essential because all sin starts with our thoughts: **"May all my thoughts be pleasing to him, for I rejoice in the Lord"** (Psalm 104:34, NLT). I am thankful that the Holy Spirit has helped me please God in my thought life. Instead of allowing ungodly or untrue thoughts to dominate my mind, I take authority over them and replace them with the truth of God's Word. I desire God's standard of righteousness because my standard is totally unacceptable, no matter how good it looks on the outside. Saints of God, we have been made the righteousness of God through Christ Jesus, so let's live right righteous! (2nd Corinthians 5:21)

What is exciting to me about living righteously is that God's Word is full of promises for those who do so. Here are a few promises that bless my life on a daily basis (KJV):

1. "I have been young, and now am old; yet have I not seen the righteous forsaken, nor His seed begging bread" (Psalm 37:25).
2. "For thou, LORD, wilt bless the righteous; with favour wilt thou compass him as with a shield" (Psalm 5:12)
3. "For the righteous Lord loveth righteousness; his countenance doth behold the upright" (Psalm 11:7).
4. "Rejoice in the Lord, O ye righteous: for praise is comely for the upright" (Psalm 33:1).
5. "The eyes of the Lord are upon the righteous, and his ears are open unto their cry" (Psalm 34:15).
6. "The righteous cry, and the Lord heareth, and delivereth them out of all their troubles" (Psalm 34:17)
7. "Many are the afflictions of the righteous: but the Lord delivereth him out of them all" (Psalm 34:19).
8. "The righteous shall flourish like the palm tree: he shall grow like a cedar in Lebanon" (Psalm 92:12).

Saints of God, there are many scriptures that focus on the blessings of living righteously. When I made the decision to conquer strongholds in my life, I experienced all of the blessings mentioned in the above scriptures. My ministry, career, health and family life have all improved. I am better off financially now than I was when the economy was booming. More than anything, the peace and glory of God are on my life so that I can be a blessing to others. People have told me there is something different about me. I know it is the glory of God, because of my deliverance from strongholds.

Before we end this chapter, I want to share with you something special the Lord revealed to me when I was preparing a message on strongholds for a women's retreat. The Lord gave me five C's as a guide to living righteously during and after conquering strongholds:

Choose: Choose your thoughts. Practice changing your thoughts to what is good, honest, lovely, pure and godly (Philippians 4:8). Choose this day who you will serve. Will it be God or your flesh (Joshua 24:15)?

Confess: Practice speaking God's Word out loud to develop new thinking patterns that agree with it. Say what God says about you in His Word. Psalm 107:2 states, **"Let the redeemed of the Lord say so, whom He hath redeemed from the hand of the enemy"** (KJV). You should not deny any stronghold-related situation occurring in your life, but you do have the ability to speak **life** to that situation and command it to line up with God's Word.

Control: Practice guarding your thoughts and being mindful of what you are thinking about. Ask yourself where you are camping out (the mind of the spirit or the mind of the flesh?). Philippians 2:5 says to **"let this mind by in you, which was also in Christ Jesus."** First Peter 1:15 reads, **"But as He which hath called you is holy, so be ye holy in all manner of conversation"** (KJV). Set your mind on things above.

Conquer: Practice using your spiritual weapons of prayer, faith, walking in love, and confessing the Word of God. Use your sword (the Word of God) as an offensive weapon against the enemy. When you speak God's Word, you **look** like God to the devil!

Celebrate: Celebrate the truth of God's Word and what He says about you. Celebrate making godly choices. The Apostle Paul enjoyed his relationship with the Lord despite difficult circumstances in ministry. He was determined to live righteously. Paul's hope was in Christ and spending eternity with Him. Celebrate where you are seated ... heavenly places in Christ Jesus (Ephesians 2:6). The world needs to see us celebrating...we have the best seat in the house (in Christ)!

Practice these five C's and see if your life does not undergo positive changes similar to those realized by these four individuals with strongholds we discussed in the Introduction to this book.

Separated from his wife and daughters, Pastor Glover spent several months blaming everyone but himself for his downfall and getting nowhere. Finally, he decided he was "sick and tired of being sick and tired," and began to study God's word with new eyes. Reading Psalm 119, where David expressed his love for God's word, really struck him. After receiving Godly counseling from a fellow minister, Pastor Glover dealt with the roots to his strongholds. As a result, he experienced a freedom and hunger for God's word that equipped him to **live** *righteous and holy. Pastor Glover once again became "strong in the Lord, and in the power of His might." He also went into counseling with his wife, won her back, and by confronting Satan with God's word; he was able to resist any further temptation to commit adultery.*

After her best friend, also a successful banker, was arrested for driving under the influence and suffered public embarrassment, Polly tearfully confessed her addiction to the Lord. He showed her that all she had to do was keep her eyes on Him; and depend on Him; and look to Him, not her job, to make her feel complete. Polly shared her struggle with her pastor, who referred her to an addictions support group within the church. The group's Bible study spurred Polly's own personal study, which became more fulfilling to her than drinking with the coworkers had ever been.

Sister Cringle's husband took her aside and told her the truth in love ... that she had earned a bad reputation in her community and church due to her negative, critical, jealous comments about anyone who God had blessed. She angrily denied it. But then one cold day she passed by a group of homeless people, including children, huddling on the side of the street. The sight of them was a startling reminder to her: She might not have some of the things other believers have, but she was no less blessed! Sister Cringle went home, got her Bible out, and began confessing key scriptures on her blessed state. Shortly thereafter she signed up to volunteer at the local homeless shelter and soup kitchen, and realized what a joy it was to serve others less fortunate than she.

Sharita couldn't take it anymore. No matter how good the sex was, it was not worth the disappointments, the embarrassments, the near-suicidal depression. One day she ran into a friend, a woman who used to be one of the wildest women in the neighborhood but who had found her Mr. Right and was happily married. The friend told Sharita that the "must have a man and fornicate with him to keep him" mentality was a dangerous stronghold and that God could help Sharita overcome that stronghold. The friend invited Sharita to her church, whose pastor was dedicated to helping each and every individual not just keep from going to hell, but walk in complete victory here on earth. Through the church's teachings, Sharita learned that God didn't forbid His children to fornicate just to keep them from having any fun; His commandments were there to protect them! She realized that the love she had to give, she was obligated to give God first ... He was her "man." She also learned that marriage was a ministry ... and that she needed to love and minister unto God before He could bless her with a husband to minister to. Sharita began to "dwell in the secret place of the Most High" and make God her everything. For the first time, she was happy without an earthly man in her life. However, a certain Godly man, who'd been praying for a wife, began to take notice ...

It is my prayer that this book has given you spiritual wisdom and insight to conquer strongholds in your life. The conquering of strongholds sets you on a path to have God's very **best** in your life. I am a living testimony of what God will do in the life of a person who is **free** to serve Him with her whole spirit, soul and body.

Although old thought patterns and sinful habits may try to resurface because of our flesh, we can quickly cast them down with the authority we have in Christ Jesus. The Apostle Paul, in Romans 8:37 (KJV), encourages me and others by saying, "Nay, in all these things we are more than conquerors through Him that loved us."

BIBLIOGRAPHY

Dupins, Prentice Sr. (March 22, 2009). "The Believer's Response to the Storm: The Secret Storm." Sermon.

Dupins, Teresia. (2009). "Children of the Day: It's no Time to Play in the Dark." Sermon.

Kimball, Josh. (February 28, 2009). *Christian Artists Address Sex "Crisis" on Tour.* Retrieved from Internet site www.christianpost.com

Leaf, Caroline. Who Switched off My Brain? Controlling Toxic Thoughts and Emotions. Switch on Your Brain Organisation Publishers, South Africa, 2007.

Life Application Study Bible: New Living Translation: 2nd Edition. Tyndale House Publishers, Inc. Wheaton, Illinois, 2004.

Merriam-Webster's Collegiate Dictionary. Available online at http://www. Merriam-WebsterCollegiate.com

Moore, Beth. Jesus: The One and Only. B&H Publishing Group. Nashville, TN, 2002.

New American Standard Bible. The Word of God Alive & Active. American Bible Society. New York, 1991.

Parallel Bible: King James Version & Amplified Bible Parallel Edition. Zondervan Publishers, Grand Rapids, Michigan, 1995.

Rollins, Roger. (March 1, 2009). *Pornography will destroy marriage, you.* Retrieved from Aikenstandard.com.

Schaumburg, H.W. False Intimacy: Understanding the Struggle of Sexual Addiction. NavPress Publishers. Colorado Springs, CO, 1993.

Schuckit, M.A. Drug and Alcohol Abuse: A Clinical Guide to Diagnosis and Treatment. Springer Science + Business Media Inc. New York, NY, 2006.

Stone, Perry. "3:00 in the Morning: Tapping into the Spirit World," (audio) Voice of Evangelism, Cleveland, TN.

Sutherland, Fraser. Random House Webster's College Thesaurus. Random House, Inc. New York, NY, 1998.

The Holy Bible. King James Version. Holman Bible Publishers, Nashville, TN 1982.

Vine, W.E., M.F. Unger and W. White Jr. Vine's Complete Expository Dictionary of Old and New Testament Word. Thomas Nelson Publishers, Nashville, TN 1996.

Youngblood, R.F., Bruce, F. F. & Harrison, R.K. Nelson's Student Bible Dictionary: A Complete Guide to Understanding the World of the Bible. Thomas Nelson Publishers Nashville, TN, 2005.

Webster's II New Riverside Desk Dictionary: Home and Office Edition. Houghton Mifflin Company, Boston, MA, 1998.

Womack, Andrew. Grace the Power of the Gospel: Study Guide. Andrew Womack Ministries, Inc. Colorado Springs, CO. 2007.

About the Author

Teresia Dupins is an ordained minister of Covenant Family Church in North Little Rock, AR, where her husband, Prentice Dupins Sr., is the pastor. Their ministry focuses on helping individuals establish a close relationship with Christ to fulfill the call of God on their lives.

She holds a Master of Science degree in nursing. In addition, she holds national certification in psychiatric nursing as well as national certification in addictions nursing. She and her husband have two grown children who are ministry leaders at Covenant Family Church.

She is also the founder and co-director of Renewed to Walk in Truth Ministries, which centers on helping women conquer strongholds in their lives by renewing their minds with the Word of God. The ministry includes weekly Bible studies, conferences and retreats to empower women with godly wisdom that transforms their lives. Women have experienced transformation and victory in their lives through participation in Renewed to Walk in Truth Ministries.

God placed in her a desire to help people in the body of Christ conquer strongholds so they may walk in truth and live victoriously. In this book, she shares her personal experience with strongholds and how God helped her conquer them. She believes this book is ordained by God to help Christians conquer strongholds that prevent them from maturing and fulfilling the call of God on their lives.

CPSIA information can be obtained at www.ICGtesting.com
Printed in the USA
LVOW13s0123290114

371331LV00002B/3/P